The National Parks Bucket List

THE ULTIMATE ADVENTURE JOURNAL FOR ALL 63 PARKS

LINDA MOHAMMAD

EPIC INK

TABLE OF CONTENTS

. . .

INTRODUCTION

. . .

WELCOME TO AMERICA'S BEST IDEA, our beloved national parks. This bucket list journal is thoughtfully curated not just for the "outdoorsy" folks, but for all the national park lovers who have made it their lifetime goal to experience what our public lands have to offer. Big trees, sand dunes, hot springs, underground caves, dark skies, kelp forest, rainforest, arches, canyons, glaciers, volcanoes, badlands, beaches, deserts, mountains, endangered species now making a comeback, you name it—our parks have it.

National parks are tightly woven into the fabric of American culture. They are iconic, rich in history, and offer a magical experience without the pixie dust. Over the decades, generations of visitors have enjoyed these stunning landscapes to marvel at wildlife, walk in the footsteps of people who came before us and shaped our history, and form connections to the outdoors. Some of that love for the great outdoors stemmed from childhood memories. For some of us, like myself, who didn't grow up "outdoorsy" or who migrated to the United States and stumbled upon these natural beauties, this is what American dreams are made of.

The birth of the national park idea was sparked in the late 1800s during the settlers' discovery of what is now known as Yellowstone National Park. Inspired by the Yosemite Act that reserved Yosemite Valley from settlement and entrusted it to the care of the state of California, the national park idea was made a reality by Congress in 1872, when President Ulysses S. Grant signed the Yellowstone National Park Protection Act into law. Then, the world's first national park was born. Almost half a century later, the idea developed into a system that, through the years, has grown to embrace more than 85 million acres of land across the United States. What started as a commercialization idea of these wonders of the world to attract tourists, the "Organic Act" was signed on August 25, 1916, by President Woodrow Wilson, creating the National Park Service—a new federal bureau in the Department of the Interior responsible for protecting our national parks and monuments.

In an era of Westward expansion, the federal government had the foresight to set aside land deemed too valuable in natural wonders to develop. Can you imagine a world without the giant sequoias or redwoods standing tall because they were consumed as timber? Or a less vibrant Grand Prismatic Springs in Yellowstone due to people throwing rocks in the pool and plugging the heat source, changing the makeup of the bacteria? Or no more condors soaring above the sky with their 10-foot wingspan as they become extinct due to habitat loss and lead poisoning? You get the gist. Conservation is critical. For the record, there are more than 420 parks that are managed by the National Park Service. Sixty-three of the "big parks" are designated as national parks, while the remaining 360+ "small parks" fall under several other designations, such as national monuments and national historical parks.

So if you're wondering, why should you visit the national parks? Simply put, your time spent at the parks will inspire curiosity and lifelong learning that can be passed on from one generation to the next. Our parks serve a vital role in preserving, protecting, and sharing some of the most important historical, geological, and cultural resources, and maintain critical ecological biodiversity. Besides instilling a sense of preservation, exposure to nature has endless benefits for our physical health and overall well-being. There is so much beauty to be experienced, feeding our craving for adventure and reigniting our tired souls as we ground ourselves through connection with the land. For me, finding these parks have been a life-changing experience for the better.

Now the real question is, why should you do it sooner rather than later? When I first started my National Parks Bucket List journey in 2016 (there were 59 national parks at the time), I set the intention to see all 59 parks before I turned 59 (I was 34 at the time). The goal was to experience these parks before I retire, and it helped motivate me to intentionally use my annual vacation time and weekends to balance the long hard days at work. Although the National Park Service keeps moving the goalpost when new parks are upgraded to national park status, at the time of writing this book, there are 63 national parks and I've been fortunate to experience them all in less than five years. As I revisited some of my favorite parks, it dawned on me that the landscape and climate are changing. Mountain slopes and badlands erode, glaciers retreat, tallest and oldest trees fall, valleys and river plains flood, and some of our greatest treasures are no longer accessible to the public due to destruction (by humans or Mother Nature). Tomorrow may become someday. Someday may become never. So why not now?

A century ago, John Muir described the entire American continent as a wild garden "favored above all the other wild parks and gardens of the globe." But in reality, the North American continent has not been a wilderness for at least 15,000 years. Many of the landscapes that became national parks had been molded and cared for by Indigenous peoples for millennia. While the creation of the national parks meant environmental conservation, it does often restrict Indigenous peoples from using their land for cultural purposes and traditional practices. We cannot fully appreciate the history of these parks without acknowledging the connection between conservation efforts and the atrocities conducted against Indigenous peoples. And to that, I urge you to adventure responsibly and respect the land that you are recreating on. Let us become stewards of the land as we continue to preserve our national parks "for the benefit and enjoyment of the people."

Now, dig into these pages and start planning your bucket list, whether that's for all of the parks or as many parks as you're able to get to. I hope this journal helps guide your way through America's Best Idea.

—Linda Mohammad, The Bucket List Traveler

HOW TO USE THIS JOURNAL

. . .

THIS JOURNAL IS INTENDED to be your carry-on companion that serves as keepsake while you explore your way through the National Parks Bucket List. The parks are divided based on their geographical locations, listed regionally from west to east, trending north to south. From the Pacific Northwest and Alaska crossing through the Rocky Mountains and the Midwest to the North Atlantic with all the other regions in between, you're sure to find unique landscapes and fascinating history that each park has to offer.

The first half of each park's profile is the quick guide section, where you'll learn the essence of the park, its reason for protection, and the information needed to inspire you to start your park planning. For the most up-to-date information, check out the official website for each park, listed at the top of the guide section, or each park's social media accounts. Looking for more information on the lodging and camping options inside the parks? Head over to my website (www.thebucketlisttraveler.com) for details.

One note about the year of each park's being established: The number refers to when it received its national park designation. About half of our current national parks gained protection as different entities within the National Park Service, such as national monuments, before being designated national parks. For those cases, the initial designated date is in parentheses for your reference. What makes this journal special (besides it being my labor of love) are the Bucket List Traveler Tips, curated based on firsthand experiences from my own National Parks Bucket List journey.

The second half of each park's profile is the journal section where you'll be prompted to jot down the following:

- Basic information of your trip, such as date, lodging/camping, and travel companions
- A blank square for you to collect your Passport to Your National Parks stamp
- Your favorite trails and views explored during the visit
- Moments captured and memories made, plus any bucket list items checked
- The park rating. This is subject to your interpretation, but if you're looking for guidance, here's mine:

  ★ ★ ★ ★ ★   ABSOLUTELY MAGICAL AND PERFECT ALL AROUND

  ★ ★ ★ ★   GREAT EXPERIENCE, MEMORIES WERE MADE

  ★ ★ ★   GOOD EXPERIENCE, COULD BE BETTER

  ★ ★   NEED BETTER PLANNING, TIMING, AND EXECUTION

  ★   WHY DID I EVEN LEAVE MY HOUSE FOR THIS?

- And finally, would you come back for a return visit? Check **Yes** or **No**!

One disclaimer that I want to mention, in the world of influencers and cryptocurrency these days: All experiences and dollars spent on each of these trips and for every single activity are my own. No sponsors, no collaborations, no payment received. As such, all suggestions on local outfitters or tour operators in the Bucket List Traveler Tips are based on personal experiences. No #ad or #gifted, period!

I would love to follow along as you journal your way through the National Parks Bucket List journey. Tag me on Instagram (@thebucketlisttraveler) or send me pictures of your journal in the wild via linda@thebucketlisttraveler.com so we can geek out over it together. Share your progress and let's celebrate your accomplishments, one park at a time!

Travel Tips

YOU MAY ALREADY BE FAMILIAR with some of these tips, but I want to ensure successful and enjoyable visits as you work your way through your bucket list! Please pass these on to friends and family, too, so that collectively we can recreate responsibly, safely, economically, and efficiently!

- Save time at the park entrance by paying your entry fee online at Recreation.gov. Once paid, download the digital pass for the entrance station or booth. Note that one paid entrance fee is valid for seven days.

- Get the annual America the Beautiful Pass. The pass is good for a year from purchase with two signatures of pass holders, covering four persons within the same party (children under 16 are always admitted free). The annual pass is a great option if you plan to visit three or more parks within a year for a break-even cost and future cost savings. There is also a lifetime senior pass. Military personnel (including veterans and Gold Star Family members) enter for free, and families with fourth graders also receive free admission through the Every Kid Outdoors program.

- Free entrance days in the national parks are offered five times a year on Martin Luther King Jr.'s birthday in January, the first day of National Park Week in April, the anniversary of the Great American Outdoors Act in August, National Public Lands Day in September, and Veterans Day in November. If you have an annual pass or are willing to pay an entrance fee, try and avoid the parks on these days to give a chance for others to enjoy the parks for free.

- Prepare for travels to remote areas where phone coverage may be sparse. Fuel your vehicle often to keep a full tank. Always inform someone where you're going, especially when traveling solo.

- Do your general research before heading to a park to help plan your activities and accommodation. Download any virtual guide, permit (timed entry, popular trails, and scenic drives), or document you may need on your phone ahead of time. The National Park Service phone application has capabilities for you to download a park's profile for use when you don't have phone service.

- Some activities may require special use permits from the park (e.g., commercial photography or videography, wedding, group, or First Amendment activities), so do some research to ensure you're in compliance.

- If traveling with children, ask park rangers about the Junior Ranger Program (adults can do it too!). If traveling with pets, check the park's policy to understand where, when, and how pets are allowed.

- Check the park's official website and social media accounts for the latest update on the park's status, events, or closures.

- Understand general park rules and recommendations and stay on designated trails except in parks that have an open-hike policy. Always leave the area better than when you found it by picking up after yourself and minimize your trace, as well as practicing proper food storage and safe wildlife viewing.

When arriving at the park, plan to stop by at the visitor center to chat with park rangers or volunteers to orient yourself and for some tips specific to the park. Please refrain from asking too many questions when entering the park entrance's booth so the incoming traffic can keep moving consistently.

This book was written from a somewhat introverted point of view. Wherever I can, I consider timing (season, day, or hour) and activity and trail choices to find opportunities to experience the park with a manageable amount of crowds.

Lastly, go find your park!

BEST OF AMERICA'S
BEST IDEA
• • •

THE NATIONAL PARK SERVICE'S 63 national parks saw nearly 89 million recreation visits in 2022. This Top 10 list is compiled based on the number of visitations per park, so perhaps it's more of a popularity list because "best" can be subjective based on experiences and memories made. After all, beauty and the "best" are in the eye of the beholder. Want to know what my Top 10 list is? Flip to the end of the book!

1. GREAT SMOKY MOUNTAINS NATIONAL PARK, 12.94 MILLION VISITORS

2. GRAND CANYON NATIONAL PARK, 4.73 MILLION VISITORS

3. ZION NATIONAL PARK, 4.69 MILLION VISITORS

4. ROCKY MOUNTAIN NATIONAL PARK, 4.3 MILLION VISITORS

5. ACADIA NATIONAL PARK, 3.97 MILLION VISITORS

6. YOSEMITE NATIONAL PARK, 3.67 MILLION VISITORS

7. YELLOWSTONE NATIONAL PARK, 3.29 MILLION VISITORS

8. JOSHUA TREE NATIONAL PARK, 3.06 MILLION VISITORS

9. CUYAHOGA VALLEY NATIONAL PARK, 2.91 MILLION VISITORS

10. GLACIER NATIONAL PARK, 2.91 MILLION VISITORS

WASHINGTON

OREGON

IDAHO

MONTANA

NORTH DAKOTA

SOUTH DAKOTA

WYOMING

NEVADA

NEBRASKA

UTAH

COLORADO

CALIFORNIA

KANSAS

ARIZONA

NEW MEXICO

OKLAHOMA

AMERICAN
SAMOA

HAWAI'I

TEXAS

ALASKA

MAINE

VERMONT

NEW HAMPSHIRE

MASSACHUSETTS

RHODE ISLAND

CONNECTICUT

NEW YORK

...SOTA

WISCONSIN

MICHIGAN

PENNSYLVANIA

NEW JERSEY

MARYLAND DELAWARE

IOWA

OHIO

INDIANA

ILLINOIS

WEST VIRGINIA

VIRGINIA

MISSOURI

KENTUCKY

NORTH CAROLINA

TENNESSEE

ARKANSAS

SOUTH CAROLINA

ALABAMA

GEORGIA

MISSISSIPPI

LOUISIANA

FLORIDA

PUERTO RICO

VIRGIN ISLANDS

NORTH ATLANTIC REGION

MID-ATLANTIC REGION

NATIONAL CAPITAL

SOUTHEAST REGION

MIDWEST REGION

SOUTHWEST REGION

ROCKY MOUNTAIN REGION

WESTERN REGION

PACIFIC NORTHWEST & ALASKA REGION

15

PACIFIC NORTHWEST

Some of the most remote and coolest (literally) national parks in the United States are located in this region, including America's largest national park. Included in this section are the national parks located in Alaska, Washington, and Oregon. Here, you'll find glimpses of the last ice age, among other rarities and superlatives, including the largest icefield in the country; the longest glacier in the entire Alaska Range; the largest active, high-latitude, sand dune field on Earth; the lowest latitude in the world in which glaciers form below an elevation of 6,500 feet; the deepest lake in America and one of the cleanest, clearest, and deepest lakes in the world; and the tallest waterfall in the continental United States.

Alaska

- [ ] KOBUK VALLEY NATIONAL PARK
- [ ] GATES OF THE ARCTIC NATIONAL PARK
- [ ] DENALI NATIONAL PARK
- [ ] LAKE CLARK NATIONAL PARK
- [ ] KATMAI NATIONAL PARK
- [ ] KENAI FJORDS NATIONAL PARK
- [ ] WRANGELL-ST. ELIAS NATIONAL PARK
- [ ] GLACIER BAY NATIONAL PARK

Washington

- [ ] NORTH CASCADES NATIONAL PARK
- [ ] OLYMPIC NATIONAL PARK
- [ ] MOUNT RAINIER NATIONAL PARK

Oregon

- [ ] CRATER LAKE NATIONAL PARK

ALASKA

GATES OF THE ARCTIC
NATIONAL PARK

KOBUK VALLEY
NATIONAL PARK

ARCTIC CIR

WRANGELL–ST. ELIAS
NATIONAL PARK

LAKE CLARK
NATIONAL PARK

KENAI FJORDS
NATIONAL PARK

GLACIER BAY
NATIONAL PARK

KATMAI
NATIONAL PARK

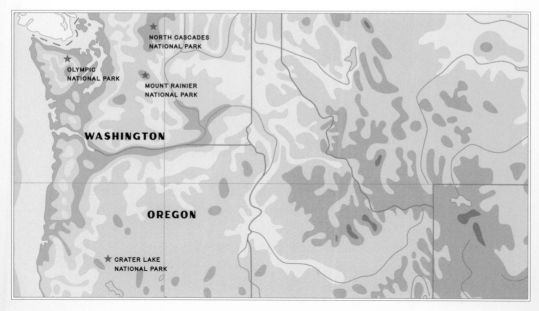

NORTH CASCADES
NATIONAL PARK

OLYMPIC
NATIONAL PARK

MOUNT RAINIER
NATIONAL PARK

WASHINGTON

OREGON

CRATER LAKE
NATIONAL PARK

KOBUK VALLEY NATIONAL PARK

ESTABLISHED: 1980 (1978) • SIZE: 2,736 SQUARE MILES • LOCATION: NORTHWESTERN ALASKA
ANCESTRAL LAND OF IÑUPIAQ AND KOYUKON ATHABASKAN PEOPLES
FOR MORE INFORMATION: NPS.GOV/KOVA

Home to almost half a million caribou that migrate through the park, Kobuk Valley sits 25 miles north of the Arctic Circle. The park provides protection for several important geographic features, including 61 miles of the central portion of Kobuk River, the 25-square-mile Great Kobuk Sand Dunes, and the Little Kobuk and Hunt River dunes. Summers are cool and cloudy with clear, cool days in September. Winters are long, frigid, snowy, windy, and partly cloudy. In spring and fall, western caribou herds cross the sand dunes during their 600-mile migration to and from their calving grounds. This is one of the last, great large mammal migrations on Earth that remains unobstructed by roads. Deserving an honorary mention is the historic Onion Portage, an important passage where the Iñupiaq people have spent significant time camping, making tools, and preparing game for more than 8,000 years.

The Bucket List Traveler Tip

TO REACH KOBUK VALLEY, I FLEW FROM FAIRBANKS INTO BETTLES, THEN HOPPED ON A FLIGHTSEEING TRIP WITH BROOKS RANGE AVIATION TO KOBUK VALLEY AND GATES OF THE ARCTIC. I RECOMMEND THIS ROUTE, AS WELL AS SPENDING THE NIGHT AT THEIR VERY AFFORDABLE RENTAL CABIN!

ADVENTURE AWAITS!

DATE(S) VISITED:

TRAVEL COMPANION(S):

WEATHER:

LODGINGS:

NATIONAL PARK PASSPORT STAMP

NATIONAL PARK PASSPORT STAMP

ON THE TRAIL

MY FAVORITE WALKS, HIKES, AND VIEWS

1.   3.

2.   4.

FLORA & FAUNA

THE MOST EXCITING PLANTS AND ANIMALS I SPOTTED ON MY TRIP

1.   3.

2.   4.

TAKE NOTHING BUT MEMORIES

MEMORABLE MOMENTS FROM MY TRIP

PARK RATING ☆ ☆ ☆ ☆ ☆   PLANNING A RETURN TRIP?   YES ☐ NO ☐

GATES OF THE ARCTIC NATIONAL PARK

ESTABLISHED: 1980 (1978) • SIZE: 13,238 SQUARE MILES • LOCATION: NORTHERN ALASKA

ANCESTRAL LAND OF THE NUNAMIUT, IÑUPIAQ AND KOYUKON ATHABASKAN PEOPLES

FOR MORE INFORMATION: NPS.GOV/GAAR

Gates of the Arctic is a roadless park located entirely north of the Arctic Circle, making it the northernmost national park in the United States. It's known for its rugged Arctic tundra landscape, seemingly endless glaciated valleys, and abundance of wildlife. Primarily visited by adventurous souls who either backpack into the park by foot or plane or travel along the handful of scenic rivers that run through the park, Gates of the Arctic sees roughly 7,000 visitors a year. Being this far north on the map, experiencing the northern lights is almost guaranteed. The park preserves the vast, expansive, wild, and virtually untouched Arctic environment, while providing opportunities for backcountry recreation and traditional subsistence uses.

The Bucket List Traveler Tip DON'T MISS THE NORTHERN LIGHTS! FOR MY GATES OF THE ARCTIC TRIP, I HAD DINNER AT THE BETTLES LODGE AND MADE FRIENDS WITH FOLKS WHO PROMISED ME A NORTHERN LIGHTS WAKE-UP CALL. THE KNOCK CAME AT 2 AM. IT WAS SIMPLY MAGICAL. BUCKET LIST CHECKED!

ADVENTURE AWAITS!

DATE(S) VISITED:

TRAVEL COMPANION(S):

WEATHER:

LODGINGS:

NATIONAL PARK PASSPORT STAMP

NATIONAL PARK PASSPORT STAMP

ON THE TRAIL

MY FAVORITE WALKS, HIKES, AND VIEWS

1.

2.

3.

4.

FLORA & FAUNA

THE MOST EXCITING PLANTS AND ANIMALS I SPOTTED ON MY TRIP

1.

2.

3.

4.

TAKE NOTHING BUT MEMORIES

MEMORABLE MOMENTS FROM MY TRIP

PARK RATING ☆ ☆ ☆ ☆ ☆

PLANNING A RETURN TRIP?

YES ☐ NO ☐

DENALI NATIONAL PARK

ESTABLISHED: 1917 • SIZE: 7,408 SQUARE MILES • LOCATION: CENTRAL ALASKA
ANCESTRAL LAND OF THE AHTNA, DENA'INA, KOYUKON, UPPER KUSKOKWIM, AND TANANA PEOPLES
FOR MORE INFORMATION: NPS.GOV/DENA

Known as Denali by the Athabaskan, this park preserves a diverse tapestry of plant life and intact ecosystems of the boreal forest and low tundra landscape. Initially created to protect Dall sheep from decimation due to market hunting and the arrival of the railroad, the park boundaries were later expanded to include protection of Denali and provide a place for wilderness recreation. Measuring 20,310 feet as the tallest peak in North America, Denali has glaciers that cover 1 million acres. It's not just the mountain that makes Denali National Park such a special place. Alaska's "Big Five"—bears, moose, caribou, wolves, and Dall sheep—are part of the 39 species of mammals that call this park home.

The Bucket List Traveler Tip BEST SPOTS TO VIEW DENALI: MILE 9 (FIRST PEEK), MILE 11 (PULL-OUT BY INTERPRETIVE WAYSIDES), MILE 12 (PARKING AREA AT MOUNTAIN VISTA, SHORT TRAIL FOR VANTAGE POINT), MILE 62 (FIRST BASE-TO-SUMMIT VIEWPOINT AT STONY DOME), AND MILE 85 BY THE REFLECTION POND (VERY EARLY IN THE MORNING OR LATE IN THE EVENING).

ADVENTURE AWAITS!

DATE(S) VISITED:

TRAVEL COMPANION(S):

WEATHER:

LODGINGS:

NATIONAL PARK PASSPORT STAMP

NATIONAL PARK PASSPORT STAMP

ON THE TRAIL

MY FAVORITE WALKS, HIKES, AND VIEWS

1.   3.

2.   4.

FLORA & FAUNA

THE MOST EXCITING PLANTS AND ANIMALS I SPOTTED ON MY TRIP

1.   3.

2.   4.

TAKE NOTHING BUT MEMORIES

MEMORABLE MOMENTS FROM MY TRIP

PARK RATING ☆ ☆ ☆ ☆ ☆   PLANNING A
                              RETURN TRIP?   YES ☐   NO ☐

LAKE CLARK NATIONAL PARK

ESTABLISHED: 1980 (1978) • SIZE: 4,093 SQUARE MILES • LOCATION: SOUTHWEST ALASKA
ANCESTRAL LAND OF THE DENA'INA PEOPLE
FOR MORE INFORMATION: NPS.GOV/LAC

Featuring a shimmering turquoise body of water, steaming volcanoes, and world-record-size lake trout and sockeye salmon, Lake Clark National Park preserves an intact ecosystem at the headwaters of the largest sockeye salmon fishery in the world. The park's glacial blue freshwater lake is the sixth-largest lake in Alaska, extending from the low rolling tundra of the Bristol Bay drainage to the high sheer peaks of the Chigmit Mountains. Ringed by these craggy cliffs, the lake runs 43 miles along scenic Alaskan terrain and plays a critical role as the birthplace for the sockeye salmon species before they venture out into the open ocean prior to making their swim back to the lake for spawning. The bear-viewing opportunities on the coast are world class, as brown bears congregate in high numbers to feed. Chinitna Bay, Crescent Lake, Silver Salmon Creek, Shelter Creek, and Tuxedni Bay are prime spots for viewing.

The Bucket List Traveler Tip THE PARK'S WEBSITE HAS AN EXTENSIVE LIST OF PERMITTED AIR TAXI OPERATORS. I WENT WITH LAKE CLARK AIR AND STAYED OVERNIGHT AT THE FARM LODGE (BOTH OWNED BY THE ALSWORTH FAMILY). IT WAS A CUSTOM PACKAGE DESIGNED TO FIT MY INTERESTS AND THEIR AVAILABILITY.

ADVENTURE AWAITS!

DATE(S) VISITED:

TRAVEL COMPANION(S):

WEATHER:

LODGINGS:

ON THE TRAIL

MY FAVORITE WALKS, HIKES, AND VIEWS

1.   3.

2.   4.

FLORA & FAUNA

THE MOST EXCITING PLANTS AND ANIMALS I SPOTTED ON MY TRIP

1.   3.

2.   4.

TAKE NOTHING BUT MEMORIES

MEMORABLE MOMENTS FROM MY TRIP

PARK RATING ☆ ☆ ☆ ☆ ☆   PLANNING A RETURN TRIP?   YES ☐   NO ☐

KATMAI NATIONAL PARK

ESTABLISHED: 1980 (1918) • SIZE: 5,741 SQUARE MILES • LOCATION: SOUTHERN ALASKA
ANCESTRAL LAND OF THE SUGPIAQ'ALUTIIQ, INUIT, YUPIK, AND DENA'INA ATHABASKAN PEOPLES
FOR MORE INFORMATION: NPS.GOV/KATM

Initially created to preserve the famed Valley of Ten Thousand Smokes—a spectacular 700-foot deep ash flow deposited by the Novarupta Volcano in 1912 that turned a green valley into the ash-filled land we see today—Katmai National Park has expanded to protect 9,000 years of human history as well as an important habitat for salmon. The park remains an active volcanic landscape, also featuring broad river flats and looming mountains, but, like Lake Clark, it is more renowned for its bear watching. One of the best bear-viewing locations is at Brooks Camp. Every fall, the park hosts Fat Bear Week, a single elimination tournament in which park staff invite their online community to compare spring and late-summer photos of bears.

The Bucket List Traveler Tip DAY TRIPPING TO KATMAI FOR THE BUCKET-LIST BEAR-VIEWING OPPORTUNITY IS DOABLE FROM KING SALMON, KODIAK, HOMER, AND ANCHORAGE. KATMAI AIR OFFERS A DAY-TOUR PACKAGE FROM ANCHORAGE TO BROOKS FALLS AND ALASKA BEAR ADVENTURES LEAVES FROM HOMER AT A LOWER COST THAN FLIGHTS FROM ANCHORAGE.

ADVENTURE AWAITS!

DATE(S) VISITED:

TRAVEL COMPANION(S):

WEATHER:

LODGINGS:

NATIONAL PARK PASSPORT STAMP

NATIONAL PARK PASSPORT STAMP

ON THE TRAIL

MY FAVORITE WALKS, HIKES, AND VIEWS

1.

2.

3.

4.

FLORA & FAUNA

THE MOST EXCITING PLANTS AND ANIMALS I SPOTTED ON MY TRIP

1.

2.

3.

4.

TAKE NOTHING BUT MEMORIES

MEMORABLE MOMENTS FROM MY TRIP

PARK RATING ☆ ☆ ☆ ☆ ☆

PLANNING A RETURN TRIP?   YES ☐   NO ☐

KENAI FJORDS NATIONAL PARK

ESTABLISHED: 1980 (1978) • SIZE: 1,047 SQUARE MILES • LOCATION: SOUTH-CENTRAL ALASKA
ANCESTRAL LAND OF THE ALUTIIQ (SUGPIAQ) PEOPLE
FOR MORE INFORMATION: NPS.GOV/KEFJ

Kenai Fjords is a rugged glacial wonderland, offering stunning scenery, incredible wildlife diversity, and phenomenal ocean adventures that get you up close to the massive walls of tidewater glaciers. Between the rocky coastlines, towering mountains, and spectacular fjords, the park preserves the coastal rainforest, fjord ecosystem, Harding Icefield, abundant wildlife, and historical and archaeological remains. Harding Icefield, one of the few remaining icefields in the country, feeds nearly three dozen glaciers flowing out of the mountains, six of them to tidewater. The park is also a welcome habitat for over 190 species of birds, both migratory and resident, such as puffins, cormorants, kittiwakes, and eagles. It's also home to orcas, otters, puffins, bears, moose, and mountain goats. During summer, park rangers offer daily informative sessions such as an Exit Glacier walk to Glacier View overlook and an Exit Glacier talk at the pavilion.

The Bucket List Traveler Tip I HIGHLY RECOMMEND HOPPING ON ALASKA RAILROAD FROM ANCHORAGE FOR A DAY TRIP TO SEWARD FOR VIEWS THAT CAN ONLY BE SEEN FROM THE TRAIN. ONCE IN SEWARD, HOP ON A BOAT TOUR (I WENT WITH MAJOR MARINE TOURS' SIX-HOUR KENAI FJORDS NATIONAL PARK CRUISE). THE TOUR WILL FINISH JUST IN TIME FOR YOU TO CATCH THE TRAIN BACK.

ADVENTURE AWAITS!

DATE(S) VISITED:

TRAVEL COMPANION(S):

WEATHER:

LODGINGS:

NATIONAL PARK PASSPORT STAMP

NATIONAL PARK PASSPORT STAMP

ON THE TRAIL

MY FAVORITE WALKS, HIKES, AND VIEWS

1.

2.

3.

4.

FLORA & FAUNA

THE MOST EXCITING PLANTS AND ANIMALS I SPOTTED ON MY TRIP

1.

2.

3.

4.

TAKE NOTHING BUT MEMORIES

MEMORABLE MOMENTS FROM MY TRIP

PARK RATING ☆ ☆ ☆ ☆ ☆

PLANNING A
RETURN TRIP?

YES ☐ NO ☐

WRANGELL–ST. ELIAS NATIONAL PARK

ESTABLISHED: 1980 (1978) • SIZE: 13,176 SQUARE MILES • LOCATION: SOUTH-CENTRAL ALASKA
ANCESTRAL LAND OF THE AHTNA, UPPER TANANA, EYAK, AND TLINGIT PEOPLES
FOR MORE INFORMATION: NPS.GOV/WRST

The Wrangell and St. Elias mountain ranges contain some of the largest volcanoes and the greatest concentration of glaciers in North America. Wrangell–St. Elias National Park stretches from one of the tallest peaks in North America—Mount St. Elias at 18,008 feet—out to the ocean on the Gulf of Alaska and preserves the natural beauty of the diverse geologic, glacial, and riparian-dominated landscapes. Here, there are no shortages of superlatives. Hubbard Glacier is the longest tidewater glacier in North America, Bagley Icefield is the largest non-polar icefield in North America, Nabesna Glacier is the longest valley glacier in the world, and Malaspina Glacier is the world's largest piedmont glacier. The best time to visit is from the end of May through mid-September, when days are long and temperatures are cool to warm. Wildflowers and mosquitoes peak in June and July, which are also the hottest months here.

The Bucket List Traveler Tip I STAYED AT MCCARTHY BED AND BREAKFAST, HALF A MILE WEST OF THE KENNICOTT RIVER FOOTBRIDGE. THEIR CABINS ARE COZY AND AFFORDABLE. IF YOU HIRE A GUIDE FOR ACTIVITIES OR TOURS, ASK IF THEY CAN PICK YOU UP ON EITHER SIDE OF THE RIVER (THERE'S A VEHICLE BRIDGE AVAILABLE FOR THE LOCAL FOLKS).

ADVENTURE AWAITS!

DATE(S) VISITED:

TRAVEL COMPANION(S):

WEATHER:

LODGINGS:

NATIONAL PARK PASSPORT STAMP

NATIONAL PARK PASSPORT STAMP

ON THE TRAIL

MY FAVORITE WALKS, HIKES, AND VIEWS

1.

2.

3.

4.

FLORA & FAUNA

THE MOST EXCITING PLANTS AND ANIMALS I SPOTTED ON MY TRIP

1.

2.

3.

4.

TAKE NOTHING BUT MEMORIES

MEMORABLE MOMENTS FROM MY TRIP

PARK RATING ☆ ☆ ☆ ☆ ☆

PLANNING A
RETURN TRIP?

YES ☐ NO ☐

GLACIER BAY NATIONAL PARK

ESTABLISHED: 1980 (1925) • SIZE: 5,131 SQUARE MILES • LOCATION: SOUTHEAST ALASKA
ANCESTRAL LAND OF THE HUNA TLINGIT PEOPLE
FOR MORE INFORMATION: NPS.GOV/GLBA

Glacier Bay National Park is home to more than 1,000 glaciers and has experienced at least four major glacial advances and retreats, resulting in the 65-mile waterway we see today. The park serves as a natural outdoor research laboratory for scientists to learn about past ice ages and to understand the impact of climate change on glaciers. The dramatic variety of plant communities ranges from barren terrain just recovering from glacial retreat to lush temperate rainforest. Glacier Bay also has a unique underwater ecosystem that displays deepwater emergence, where marine organisms typically found in deeper parts of the ocean—such as red tree corals, anemones, and certain fish—exist here at shallower depths. The main visitor season is from late May to early September, peaking in July with good weather. As waves and tides slowly erode the ice fronts, massive blocks of ice break off and crash into the sea, resulting in once-in-a-lifetime sights—and sounds.

The Bucket List Traveler Tip IS YOUR GOAL TO SEE AS MANY NATIONAL PARKS AS YOU CAN IN ONE TRIP WHILE IN ALASKA? HERE'S A SAMPLE ITINERARY: FROM ANCHORAGE, VISIT LAKE CLARK AND KATMAI, THEN TAKE THE TRAIN TO SEWARD FOR KENAI FJORDS. FLY TO JUNEAU FROM ANCHORAGE AND CATCH A CONNECTION TO GUSTAVUS FOR GLACIER BAY. FLY BACK TO ANCHORAGE AND RENT A CAR TO DRIVE TO WRANGELL–ST. ELIAS. SWING BY KENAI FJORDS AGAIN TO HIKE TO EXIT GLACIER BEFORE HEADING HOME.

ADVENTURE AWAITS!

DATE(S) VISITED:

TRAVEL COMPANION(S):

WEATHER:

LODGINGS:

ON THE TRAIL

MY FAVORITE WALKS, HIKES, AND VIEWS

1.   3.

2.   4.

FLORA & FAUNA

THE MOST EXCITING PLANTS AND ANIMALS I SPOTTED ON MY TRIP

1.   3.

2.   4.

TAKE NOTHING BUT MEMORIES

MEMORABLE MOMENTS FROM MY TRIP

PARK RATING ☆ ☆ ☆ ☆ ☆   PLANNING A RETURN TRIP?   YES ☐   NO ☐

NORTH CASCADES NATIONAL PARK

ESTABLISHED: 1968 • SIZE: 789 SQUARE MILES • LOCATION: NORTH WASHINGTON
ANCESTRAL LAND OF THE UPPER SKAGIT, CHILLIWACK, LOWER THOMPSON, AND CHELAN PEOPLES
FOR MORE INFORMATION: NPS.GOV/NOCA

Known as the American Alps, the North Cascades preserve the jagged peaks, deep valleys, and cascading waterfalls within the unique mountainous region it encompasses. Mining and logging were once conducted in this part of Washington, threatening a pristine landscape covered with vast forests, alpine meadows, and snowfields. The park is home to more than 300 lakes and more than 300 glaciers, the largest glacial system in the United States outside Alaska. Some of the nation's finest alpine wilderness is protected under the North Cascades National Park Complex, composed of the national park itself and two national recreation areas, Ross Lake and Lake Chelan. The best weather for visiting the North Cascades generally occurs between mid-June and late September, as the park receives incredible amounts of snowfall each winter.

The Bucket List Traveler Tip WINTHROP IS A SOLID OPTION FOR YOUR BASE CAMP IF YOU'RE PLANNING TO EXPLORE THE PARK FOR SEVERAL DAYS. IT'S CLOSER TO MOST OF THE ATTRACTIONS IN THE PARK, INCLUDING THE WASHINGTON PASS OVERLOOK, MAPLE PASS, AND BLUE LAKE, ROUGHLY A 25- TO 30-MINUTE DRIVE.

ADVENTURE AWAITS!

DATE(S) VISITED:

TRAVEL COMPANION(S):

WEATHER:

LODGINGS:

NATIONAL PARK PASSPORT STAMP

NATIONAL PARK PASSPORT STAMP

ON THE TRAIL

MY FAVORITE WALKS, HIKES, AND VIEWS

1.
2.

3.
4.

FLORA & FAUNA

THE MOST EXCITING PLANTS AND ANIMALS I SPOTTED ON MY TRIP

1.
2.

3.
4.

TAKE NOTHING BUT MEMORIES

MEMORABLE MOMENTS FROM MY TRIP

PARK RATING ☆ ☆ ☆ ☆ ☆

PLANNING A RETURN TRIP?

YES ☐ NO ☐

OLYMPIC NATIONAL PARK

ESTABLISHED: 1938 (1909) • SIZE: 1,442 SQUARE MILES • LOCATION: COASTAL WASHINGTON
ANCESTRAL LAND OF THE HOH, JAMESTOWN S'KLALLAM, ELWHA KLALLAM, MAKAH, PORT GAMBLE
S'KLALLAM, QUILEUTE, QUINAULT, AND SKOKOMISH PEOPLES
FOR MORE INFORMATION: NPS.GOV/OLYM

Home to 60 named glaciers, Olympic National Park shelters three distinct ecosystems: glaciated mountains, rugged Pacific coastline, and prolific temperate rainforests. Over 95 percent of the park is designated as "wilderness," protecting one of the largest relatively untouched areas in the Lower 48, with 1,000-year-old cedar trees juxtaposed with supreme alpine meadows, pristine glacial lakes, and a vast roadless interior. The park is home to endemic species like the Olympic marmot and the Olympic torrent salamander. The best time to visit Olympic National Park is July through August, when temperatures are warm, roads and facilities are open, and a full range of programs are available. Several festivals take place within the gateway communities, including the Annual Razor Clam Digging at Kalaloch Beach, the Juan de Fuca Festival of the Arts and the Dungeness Crab & Seafood Festival in Port Angeles, Forever Twilight in Forks (for *Twilight* fans!), and the Lavender Festival in Sequim.

The Bucket List Traveler Tip
MY FIRST TIME CAMPING HERE IN APRIL, IT RAINED ALL WEEKEND. EVERYTHING WAS SOAKED, SO I COULDN'T GET THE CAMPFIRE TO START, AND I REMEMBER DRIVING INTO THE CAMPGROUND FEELING FOOLISH FOR NOT BEING PREPARED FOR THE PNW WEATHER WHILE EVERYBODY ELSE THERE HAD TARPS TO MAKE SHELTERS. DON'T BE LIKE ME!

ADVENTURE AWAITS!

DATE(S) VISITED:

TRAVEL COMPANION(S):

WEATHER:

LODGINGS:

NATIONAL PARK PASSPORT STAMP

NATIONAL PARK PASSPORT STAMP

ON THE TRAIL

MY FAVORITE WALKS, HIKES, AND VIEWS

1.   3.

2.   4.

FLORA & FAUNA

THE MOST EXCITING PLANTS AND ANIMALS I SPOTTED ON MY TRIP

1.   3.

2.   4.

TAKE NOTHING BUT MEMORIES

MEMORABLE MOMENTS FROM MY TRIP

PARK RATING ☆ ☆ ☆ ☆ ☆   PLANNING A RETURN TRIP?   YES ☐ NO ☐

MOUNT RAINIER NATIONAL PARK

ESTABLISHED: 1899 • SIZE: 369 SQUARE MILES • LOCATION: WESTERN WASHINGTON
ANCESTRAL LAND OF THE COWLITZ, MUCKLESHOOT, NISQUALLY, PUYALLUP,
SQUAXIN ISLAND, YAKAMA, AND COAST SALISH PEOPLES
FOR MORE INFORMATION: NPS.GOV/MORA

Known as Tahoma (meaning "snow-covered mountain") by the Indigenous peoples from time immemorial, Mount Rainier is the highest volcanic peak in the Lower 48. Standing 14,410 feet tall, Mount Rainier has the largest alpine glacial system outside Alaska and the world's largest volcanic glacier cave system within the summit crater. This active volcano last erupted about 150 years ago. Mount Rainier National Park, one of the oldest national parks (established prior to the creation of the National Park Service!), was established to preserve a unique forest, field, and glacial landscape under threat from the timber and mining extraction that had already ravaged much of the American West. Visitation peaks in July and August, when wildflowers transform the park's subalpine meadows and the Skip the long entrance line by staying in the park or have a backup plan to wait it out. Crystal Mountain Resort is a great option to view Mount Rainier from a higher elevation outside the park. Take their scenic gondola to the summit for an unparalleled view of the Cascade Range. In July and August, dry, warm weather provides optimal hiking conditions.

> **The Bucket List Traveler Tip** SKIP THE LONG ENTRANCE LINE BY STAYING IN THE PARK OR HAVE A BACKUP PLAN TO WAIT IT OUT. CRYSTAL MOUNTAIN RESORT IS A GREAT OPTION TO VIEW MOUNT RAINIER FROM A HIGHER ELEVATION OUTSIDE THE PARK. TAKE THEIR SCENIC GONDOLA TO THE SUMMIT FOR AN UNPARALLELED VIEW OF THE CASCADE RANGE.

ADVENTURE AWAITS!

DATE(S) VISITED:

TRAVEL COMPANION(S):

WEATHER:

LODGINGS:

NATIONAL PARK PASSPORT STAMP

NATIONAL PARK PASSPORT STAMP

ON THE TRAIL

MY FAVORITE WALKS, HIKES, AND VIEWS

1.   3.

2.   4.

FLORA & FAUNA

THE MOST EXCITING PLANTS AND ANIMALS I SPOTTED ON MY TRIP

1.   3.

2.   4.

TAKE NOTHING BUT MEMORIES

MEMORABLE MOMENTS FROM MY TRIP

PARK RATING ☆ ☆ ☆ ☆ ☆   PLANNING A RETURN TRIP?   YES ☐ NO ☐

CRATER LAKE NATIONAL PARK

ESTABLISHED: 1902 • SIZE: 286 SQUARE MILES • LOCATION: SOUTHERN OREGON
ANCESTRAL LAND OF THE KLAMATH (MAKALAK) PEOPLE
FOR MORE INFORMATION: NPS.GOV/CRLA

The deepest lake in the United States lies inside a caldera created when the 12,000-foot-high Mount Mazama collapsed 7,700 years ago following a large volcanic eruption. Rain and snowmelt accumulated in the caldera, forming Crater Lake, a lake more than 1,900 feet deep. The lake's remarkable brilliant blue color is magnified by its contrast with the ochre and rust hues of the surrounding volcanic rock walls. The intensity of this color results from the reflection of blue and green light waves off the clear water due to the absence of suspended sediment that usually would come when a body of water is fed by a stream. Summers at Crater Lake are short but sunny and the full Rim Drive loop is usually open from early July to late October. September means it's huckleberry pie season!

The Bucket List Traveler Tip HALF THE BOAT TICKETS TO WIZARD ISLAND ARE RESERVABLE AHEAD OF TIME AND THE REST CAN BE PURCHASED IN PERSON 24 HOURS PRIOR TO DEPARTURE. GETTING TO THE DOCK IS THE EASIEST PART OF THE DAY, DESCENDING 700 FEET TO THE LAKESHORE VIA CLEETWOOD COVE TRAIL.

ADVENTURE AWAITS!

DATE(S) VISITED:

TRAVEL COMPANION(S):

WEATHER:

LODGINGS:

NATIONAL PARK PASSPORT STAMP

NATIONAL PARK PASSPORT STAMP

ON THE TRAIL

MY FAVORITE WALKS, HIKES, AND VIEWS

1.   3.

2.   4.

FLORA & FAUNA

THE MOST EXCITING PLANTS AND ANIMALS I SPOTTED ON MY TRIP

1.   3.

2.   4.

TAKE NOTHING BUT MEMORIES

MEMORABLE MOMENTS FROM MY TRIP

PARK RATING ☆ ☆ ☆ ☆ ☆

PLANNING A RETURN TRIP?   YES ☐   NO ☐

WEST

When it comes to quality, quantity, and diversity of national parks in the United States, the west side is indeed the best side. Included in this section are the national parks located in California, Nevada, Arizona, Hawai'i, and American Samoa. Boasting 16 national parks and a number of superlatives—such as lowest point in North America, highest mountain peak in the Lower 48, tallest waterfall in North America, largest known tree by volume, world's tallest known tree, largest canyon in the United States, largest active volcano on Earth, biggest mountains in the world when measured from base to top—as well as being home to some of the world's oldest living organisms and petrified woods that are millions of years old, this region has a lot to offer.

California

- [ ] REDWOOD NATIONAL PARK
- [ ] LASSEN VOLCANIC NATIONAL PARK
- [ ] YOSEMITE NATIONAL PARK
- [ ] KINGS CANYON NATIONAL PARK
- [ ] SEQUOIA NATIONAL PARK
- [ ] PINNACLES NATIONAL PARK
- [ ] DEATH VALLEY NATIONAL PARK
- [ ] CHANNEL ISLANDS NATIONAL PARK
- [ ] JOSHUA TREE NATIONAL PARK

Nevada

- [ ] GREAT BASIN NATIONAL PARK

Arizona

- [ ] GRAND CANYON NATIONAL PARK
- [ ] PETRIFIED FOREST NATIONAL PARK
- [ ] SAGUARO NATIONAL PARK

Hawai'i

- [ ] HALEAKALĀ NATIONAL PARK
- [ ] HAWAI'I VOLCANOES NATIONAL PARK

American Samoa

- [ ] NATIONAL PARK OF AMERICAN SAMOA

AMERICAN SAMOA

★ NATIONAL PARK OF
AMERICAN SAMOA

165

HALEAKALĀ
NATIONAL PARK
★

0°

HAWAI'I

HAWAI'I
VOLCANOES
NATIONAL PARK
★

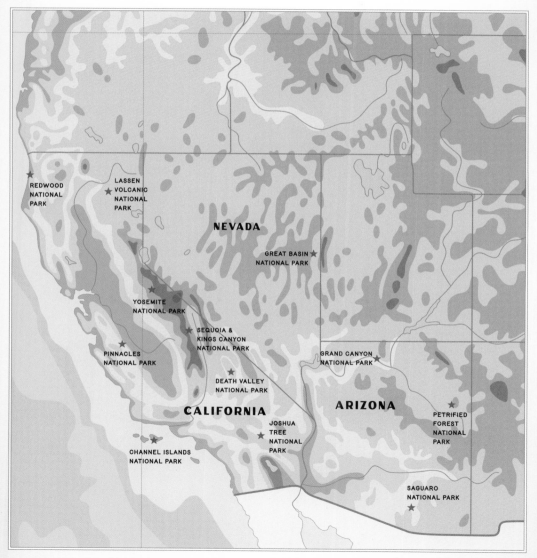

★ REDWOOD
NATIONAL
PARK

LASSEN
★ VOLCANIC
NATIONAL
PARK

NEVADA

GREAT BASIN ★
NATIONAL PARK

YOSEMITE
★ NATIONAL PARK

SEQUOIA &
★ KINGS CANYON
NATIONAL PARK

★ PINNACLES
NATIONAL PARK

DEATH VALLEY ★
NATIONAL PARK

GRAND CANYON
NATIONAL PARK ★

CALIFORNIA

ARIZONA

JOSHUA
TREE
★ NATIONAL
PARK

PETRIFIED
★ FOREST
NATIONAL
PARK

CHANNEL ISLANDS
NATIONAL PARK

SAGUARO
NATIONAL PARK
★

REDWOOD NATIONAL PARK

ESTABLISHED: 1968 • SIZE: 206 SQUARE MILES • LOCATION: NORTHERN CALIFORNIA COAST
ANCESTRAL LAND OF THE YUROK, HUPA, TOLOWA, AND KARUK PEOPLES
FOR MORE INFORMATION: NPS.GOV/REDW

Home to the tallest trees on Earth and rich in history dating back to the early days of the Indigenous peoples inhabiting the coastal redwood region, Redwood National and State Parks are co-managed by both the state of California and the federal government due to the proximity of the parks' borders. When western expansion met the redwoods in 1800s, the tall giants began to fall to a seemingly inexhaustible lumber supply that reduced the vast forests to 4 percent of the original old-growth forest within 100 years. Today, the parks preserve these redwood groves and are open to visitors year-round (though spring is the best time to visit, when the woods are at their most lush and green). In the summer, the parks conduct kayak tours of the Smith River, the largest free-flowing river system in California.

The Bucket List Traveler Tip IF YOU'RE ONLY DOING ONE HIKE HERE, THE LADY BIRD JOHNSON GROVE TRAIL (1.5-MILE LOOP) WOULD BE MY RECOMMENDATION. THIS TRAIL IS ONE OF THE FEW AREAS WHERE, WITH JUST A FEW STEPS, YOU CAN PASS THROUGH A SECOND-GROWTH FOREST (PLANTED AFTER ANCIENT REDWOODS WERE LOGGED) INTO AN OLD-GROWTH REDWOOD FOREST.

ADVENTURE AWAITS!

DATE(S) VISITED:

TRAVEL COMPANION(S):

WEATHER:

LODGINGS:

NATIONAL PARK PASSPORT STAMP

NATIONAL PARK PASSPORT STAMP

ON THE TRAIL

MY FAVORITE WALKS, HIKES, AND VIEWS

1.

2.

3.

4.

FLORA & FAUNA

THE MOST EXCITING PLANTS AND ANIMALS I SPOTTED ON MY TRIP

1.

2.

3.

4.

TAKE NOTHING BUT MEMORIES

MEMORABLE MOMENTS FROM MY TRIP

PARK RATING ☆ ☆ ☆ ☆ ☆

PLANNING A
RETURN TRIP?

YES ☐ NO ☐

LASSEN VOLCANIC NATIONAL PARK

ESTABLISHED: 1916 • SIZE: 166 SQUARE MILES • LOCATION: NORTHERN CALIFORNIA
ANCESTRAL LAND OF THE ATSUGEWI, YANA, YAHI, AND MOUNTAIN MAIDU PEOPLES
FOR MORE INFORMATION: NPS.GOV/LAVO

Mount Lassen's last eruption episode, between 1914 and 1917, changed the landscape of the area. The active volcanic landscape serves as a valuable natural laboratory of volcanic events and hydrothermal features. Lassen Volcanic National Park is among a few places in the world where all four types of volcanoes—shield, composite (stratovolcano), cinder cone, and plug dome—exist within park boundaries. Lassen Peak is the largest plug dome volcano in the world, with a peak elevation of 10,457 feet. The park is also covered with large lava pinnacles, rugged craters, steaming vents, hot springs, geysers, cinder cones, and massive lava plateaus. Far from the light pollution of civilization, Lassen is one of the last sanctuaries of natural darkness. The annual Dark Sky Festival takes place in August, with a range of activities with astrobiologists and astronomers.

The Bucket List Traveler Tip LASSEN IS MY FAVORITE OF THE CALIFORNIA NATIONAL PARKS. IT CAN BE LEISURELY ENJOYED BY CAR ALONG THE SCENIC DRIVES AND ROAD PULLOUTS, BUT IS BEST EXPERIENCED ON FOOT. LOOKING FOR A GEEKY BUCKET LIST? HIKE ALL THE FOUR VOLCANO TYPES AT CINDER CONE, LASSEN PEAK, BROKEOFF MOUNTAIN, AND PROSPECT PEAK TRAILS.

ADVENTURE AWAITS!

DATE(S) VISITED:

TRAVEL COMPANION(S):

WEATHER:

LODGINGS:

ON THE TRAIL

MY FAVORITE WALKS, HIKES, AND VIEWS

1.   3.

2.   4.

FLORA & FAUNA

THE MOST EXCITING PLANTS AND ANIMALS I SPOTTED ON MY TRIP

1.   3.

2.   4.

TAKE NOTHING BUT MEMORIES

MEMORABLE MOMENTS FROM MY TRIP

PARK RATING ☆ ☆ ☆ ☆ ☆   PLANNING A RETURN TRIP?   YES ☐   NO ☐

YOSEMITE NATIONAL PARK

ESTABLISHED: 1890 • SIZE: 1,169 SQUARE MILES • LOCATION: SIERRA NEVADA, NORTHERN CALIFORNIA

ANCESTRAL LAND OF THE AHWAHNEECHEE PEOPLE FROM THE SOUTHERN SIERRA MIWOK

FOR MORE INFORMATION: NPS.GOV/YOSE

High cliffs, deep valleys, tall waterfalls, and granite monoliths—Yosemite is simply iconic. Though Yellowstone is known as the first national park, Yosemite actually has the distinction of being the first scenic natural area set aside by the federal government for public benefit when President Lincoln signed the Yosemite Grant in 1864. Petitions for Yosemite to become a national park began in 1889, when John Muir came to the valley, and the rest is history. Another first at Yosemite is the role of Buffalo Soldiers as park rangers, patrolling the park to protect against poaching of wildlife, preventing private livestock from grazing on federal lands, and building roads and trails. The first female NPS park ranger also worked here in 1918. Millions of people visit Yosemite from April through October, though one of the most sought-after experiences is the Firefall phenomenon in February, when the sunset lights Horsetail Fall aglow.

The Bucket List Traveler Tip TO AVOID CROWDS, START EARLY IN YOSEMITE VALLEY AND END YOUR DAY OUTSIDE THE VALLEY. FROM SPRING THROUGH FALL, ARRIVE BEFORE 8 A.M. OR AFTER 5 P.M. TO MINIMIZE DELAYS AND TRAFFIC CONGESTION, AND USE THE FREE SHUTTLE TO MOVE WITHIN THE VALLEY TO SAVE YOURSELF FRUSTRATION WITH PARKING AND DRIVING SITUATIONS.

ADVENTURE AWAITS!

DATE(S) VISITED:

TRAVEL COMPANION(S):

WEATHER:

LODGINGS:

NATIONAL PARK PASSPORT STAMP
NATIONAL PARK PASSPORT STAMP

ON THE TRAIL

MY FAVORITE WALKS, HIKES, AND VIEWS

1.   3.

2.   4.

FLORA & FAUNA

THE MOST EXCITING PLANTS AND ANIMALS I SPOTTED ON MY TRIP

1.   3.

2.   4.

TAKE NOTHING BUT MEMORIES

MEMORABLE MOMENTS FROM MY TRIP

PARK RATING ☆ ☆ ☆ ☆ ☆

PLANNING A RETURN TRIP?   YES ☐   NO ☐

KINGS CANYON
NATIONAL PARK

ESTABLISHED: 1940 • SIZE: 722 SQUARE MILES • LOCATION: CENTRAL-EAST CALIFORNIA
ANCESTRAL LAND OF THE MONO AND YOKUT PEOPLES
FOR MORE INFORMATION: NPS.GOV/SEKI

Carved by glaciers during the Pleistocene Ice Age, Kings Canyon features canyon walls that reach heights of 8,200 feet, making it deeper than Grand Canyon. More than 1,000 species of vegetation, such as fir, ponderosa pine, sugar pine, cedar, mountain hemlock, and of course sequoia, call this place home, including the second-largest tree in the world, the General Grant Tree. Summer is a popular time to visit, when the Kings Canyon floor is open to traffic, but if you hope to miss the crowds, go in May or September. Winter and early spring are magical times at the park, but be prepared for snow and bring tire chains. The Dark Sky Festival takes place in September; on winter weekends there are free ranger-guided snowshoe walks (reservation required).

The Bucket List Traveler Tip DEDICATE ONE DAY TO EXPERIENCE THE CANYON'S FLOOR. THE ROUND-TRIP SCENIC DRIVE BETWEEN GRANT GROVE (6,500 FEET) AND CEDAR GROVE (4,500 FEET) ALONG THE WINDING ROAD CAN TAKE A LITTLE TIME, BETWEEN TRAFFIC AND ROADSIDE STOPS.

ADVENTURE AWAITS!

DATE(S) VISITED:

TRAVEL COMPANION(S):

NATIONAL PARK PASSPORT STAMP

NATIONAL PARK PASSPORT STAMP

WEATHER:

LODGINGS:

ON THE TRAIL

MY FAVORITE WALKS, HIKES, AND VIEWS

1.   3.

2.   4.

FLORA & FAUNA

THE MOST EXCITING PLANTS AND ANIMALS I SPOTTED ON MY TRIP

1.   3.

2.   4.

TAKE NOTHING BUT MEMORIES

MEMORABLE MOMENTS FROM MY TRIP

PARK RATING ☆ ☆ ☆ ☆ ☆   **PLANNING A RETURN TRIP?**   YES ☐ NO ☐

SEQUOIA NATIONAL PARK

ESTABLISHED: 1890 • SIZE: 631 SQUARE MILES • LOCATION: CENTRAL-EAST CALIFORNIA
ANCESTRAL LAND OF THE FOOTHILL YOKUT, TUBATULABAL, PAIUTE,
AND WESTERN MONO (MONACHE) PEOPLES

Home to the largest trees (by volume) on Earth and the highest peak in the continental United States (Mount Whitney at 14,494 feet), Sequoia National Park is named after *Sequoiadendron giganteum* trees, a species that grows naturally only on the western slopes of the Sierra Nevada between an elevation of 5,000 and 8,000 feet. These giant sequoias average from 180 to 250 feet tall and can live for more than 3,000 years, thanks to a chemical in their bark called tannin that protects against rot, boring insects, and fire. The park's most famous resident, the General Sherman Tree, is 275 feet tall, 36 feet in diameter at its base, and weighs approximately 4 million pounds. Sequoia National Park is one of the darkest places in the United States and hosts, along with its sister park Kings Canyon, the annual Dark Sky Festival in September.

The Bucket List Traveler Tip GIANT FOREST IS MY PERSONAL FAVORITE AREA OF SEQUOIA, ESPECIALLY THE DRAMATIC WELCOME FROM THE FOUR GUARDSMEN. BE IT WINTER, SPRING, SUMMER, OR FALL, THIS AREA OFFERS A DIFFERENT EXPERIENCE EACH TIME, INCLUDING A HIGH CHANCE OF RUNNING INTO BEARS MUNCHING IN ROUND MEADOW DURING SUMMERTIME.

ADVENTURE AWAITS!

DATE(S) VISITED:
....

TRAVEL COMPANION(S):
....

....

WEATHER:
....

LODGINGS:
....

NATIONAL PARK PASSPORT STAMP

NATIONAL PARK PASSPORT STAMP

ON THE TRAIL

MY FAVORITE WALKS, HIKES, AND VIEWS

1. ....   3. ....

2. ....   4. ....

FLORA & FAUNA

THE MOST EXCITING PLANTS AND ANIMALS I SPOTTED ON MY TRIP

1. ....   3. ....

2. ....   4. ....

TAKE NOTHING BUT MEMORIES

MEMORABLE MOMENTS FROM MY TRIP

....

....

....

....

....

....

....

....

....

....

....

PARK RATING ☆ ☆ ☆ ☆ ☆   **PLANNING A RETURN TRIP?**   YES ☐   NO ☐

PINNACLES NATIONAL PARK

ESTABLISHED: 2013 (1908) • SIZE: 42 SQUARE MILES • LOCATION: CENTRAL CALIFORNIA
ANCESTRAL LAND OF THE CHALON AND MUTSUN PEOPLES
FOR MORE INFORMATION: NPS.GOV/PINN

Located near the San Andreas Fault along the boundary of the Pacific Plate and the North American Plate, Pinnacles National Park is a prime example of landscape originated by tectonic plate movement. The Pinnacles volcanic field was born 23 million years ago. As it traveled along the San Andreas Fault, the field sank beneath the surface. In time, combined with the power of weathering, the old volcanic field was unearthed. These are the Pinnacles spires we see today. Fault action and earthquakes account for Pinnacles' talus caves, formed when large chunks of boulders fell into deep, narrow gorges and lodged between rock walls, forming the roofs of caves that house several bat species. The park has a Mediterranean climate, with hot, dry summers and mild winters with moderate precipitation, and springtime (March through May) is peak season for visitation, when the flowers are blooming, the talus caves are open, and the temperature is just right.

The Bucket List Traveler Tip WHEN IT COMES TO SCORING A PARKING SPOT BY BEAR GULCH DAY USE AREA, EARLY BIRDS REALLY DO GET THE WORMS. RANGERS HOLD TRAFFIC COMING INTO THE PARK UNTIL SPACES BECOME AVAILABLE, SO ARRIVING BEFORE 8 A.M. ON WEEKENDS, HOLIDAYS, AND IN SPRING CAN SAVE YOU SOME WAIT TIME.

ADVENTURE AWAITS!

DATE(S) VISITED:

TRAVEL COMPANION(S):

WEATHER:

LODGINGS:

ON THE TRAIL

MY FAVORITE WALKS, HIKES, AND VIEWS

1.   3.

2.   4.

FLORA & FAUNA

THE MOST EXCITING PLANTS AND ANIMALS I SPOTTED ON MY TRIP

1.   3.

2.   4.

TAKE NOTHING BUT MEMORIES

MEMORABLE MOMENTS FROM MY TRIP

PARK RATING ☆ ☆ ☆ ☆ ☆   PLANNING A RETURN TRIP?   YES ☐   NO ☐

DEATH VALLEY NATIONAL PARK

ESTABLISHED: 1994 (1933) • SIZE: 5,312 SQUARE MILES • LOCATION: EASTERN CALIFORNIA AND NEVADA
ANCESTRAL LAND OF THE TIMBISHA SHOSHONE PEOPLE
FOR MORE INFORMATION: NPS.GOV/DEVA

Though it is a land of the extremes, from the hottest place on Earth to the lowest point in North America, don't let the morbid name fool you: Death Valley will bring your sense of imagination to life. The park is home to almost 100 species of animals and 1,000 species of plants. It's the largest national park in the Lower 48, full of sand dunes, salt flats, racing rocks, volcanic craters, and pupfish. Created to protect against mining activities, Death Valley is also the first desert national park, redefining the idea of a landscape worth protecting. Cooler winter months are preferred for endless exploration. The skies here are virtually free of light pollution, so stars can be seen by the thousands.

The Bucket List Traveler Tip STAYING IN THE FURNACE CREEK AREA IS STRATEGIC FOR EASY ACCESS TO DIFFERENT PARTS OF THE PARK. DEATH VALLEY WAS THE PARK WHERE I KICKED OFF MY NATIONAL PARKS BUCKET LIST. I PAY HOMAGE TO IT BY RETURNING EVERY APRIL FOR WHAT I CALL THE "PARKNIVERSARY" TRIP.

ADVENTURE AWAITS!

DATE(S) VISITED:

TRAVEL COMPANION(S):

WEATHER:

LODGINGS:

NATIONAL PARK PASSPORT STAMP

NATIONAL PARK PASSPORT STAMP

ON THE TRAIL

MY FAVORITE WALKS, HIKES, AND VIEWS

1.

2.

3.

4.

FLORA & FAUNA

THE MOST EXCITING PLANTS AND ANIMALS I SPOTTED ON MY TRIP

1.

2.

3.

4.

TAKE NOTHING BUT MEMORIES

MEMORABLE MOMENTS FROM MY TRIP

PARK RATING ☆ ☆ ☆ ☆ ☆

PLANNING A
RETURN TRIP?

YES ☐ NO ☐

CHANNEL ISLANDS NATIONAL PARK

ESTABLISHED: 1980 • SIZE: 390 SQUARE MILES • LOCATION: OFF THE SOUTHERN CALIFORNIA COAST
ANCESTRAL LAND OF THE CHUMASH PEOPLE
FOR MORE INFORMATION: NPS.GOV/CHIS

Our very own Galápagos Islands are right off the coast of Southern California. More than 1,000 species of marine organisms can be found at Channel Islands National Park, which protects five of the eight Channel Islands. Santa Cruz Island is the biggest of the five, followed by Santa Rosa Island, San Miguel Island, Anacapa Island, and Santa Barbara Island. These islands were created by tectonic forces that caused them to rise up from the ocean approximately 5 million years ago. These islands have always been separated from the mainland, which explains why they have unique plants and animals there that are found nowhere else on Earth, like the island fox, once an endangered species that has now recovered thanks to the effort of the parks' recovery program. Summer and early fall are popular times to visit, when weather is ideal for water activities; winter provides the best sunsets.

The Bucket List Traveler Tip ANACAPA AND SANTA CRUZ ISLANDS ARE THE BEST OPTIONS FOR A DAY TRIP. CHOOSE ANACAPA IF YOU WANT LESS HIKING AND MORE VIEWING OR BIRDING. CHOOSE SANTA CRUZ IF YOU WANT TO COVER MORE GROUND ON TRAILS AND SEE THE ISLAND FOX IN REAL LIFE. BOTH ISLANDS HAVE GUIDED KAYAK TOURS AVAILABLE.

ADVENTURE AWAITS!

DATE(S) VISITED:

TRAVEL COMPANION(S):

WEATHER:

LODGINGS:

NATIONAL PARK PASSPORT STAMP

NATIONAL PARK PASSPORT STAMP

ON THE TRAIL

MY FAVORITE WALKS, HIKES, AND VIEWS

1.   3.

2.   4.

FLORA & FAUNA

THE MOST EXCITING PLANTS AND ANIMALS I SPOTTED ON MY TRIP

1.   3.

2.   4.

TAKE NOTHING BUT MEMORIES

MEMORABLE MOMENTS FROM MY TRIP

PARK RATING ☆ ☆ ☆ ☆ ☆   PLANNING A RETURN TRIP?   YES ☐   NO ☐

JOSHUA TREE NATIONAL PARK

ESTABLISHED: 1994 • SIZE: 1,250 SQUARE MILES • LOCATION: SOUTHERN CALIFORNIA
ANCESTRAL LAND OF THE CAHUILLA, MOJAVE, CHEMEHUEVI (SOUTHERN PAIUTE),
WESTERN SHOSHONE, AND SERRANO PEOPLES
FOR MORE INFORMATION: NPS.GOV/JOTR

Joshua trees are not actually trees—they're members of the Agave family. But in their dry desert ecosystems, these spiny *Yucca brevifolia* plants are fondly considered "trees" of the desert. Joshua Tree National Park lies at the intersection of two deserts, the Mojave and the Colorado. The "trees" are critical to the ecosystem, as they provide food and habitat to local species. Indigenous peoples recognize their usefulness, weaving the leaves into baskets and sandals, and adding flower buds and seeds to their diet. More than 50 species of mammals, 40 species of reptiles, and 700 species of plants have been identified in the park. It's a monzogranite rock wonderland for climbers, geologists, and desert dwellers alike. Take advantage of the frequent free activities in the park to learn about Joshua trees, geology, and rock climbing, or take a ranger-guided tour of Keys Ranch (fee required).

The Bucket List Traveler Tip SKIP THE WEST ENTRANCE AND ENTER THE PARK VIA THE NORTH ENTRANCE. IT'S WORTH THE EXTRA 16-MILE DRIVE TO SKIP THE LONG LINE AT THE WEST ENTRANCE. PRO TIP: AVOID VISITING THE PARK DURING COACHELLA WEEKEND FOR THE OPTIMAL EXPERIENCE!

ADVENTURE AWAITS!

DATE(S) VISITED:

TRAVEL COMPANION(S):

WEATHER:

LODGINGS:

NATIONAL PARK PASSPORT STAMP

NATIONAL PARK PASSPORT STAMP

ON THE TRAIL

MY FAVORITE WALKS, HIKES, AND VIEWS

1.   3.

2.   4.

FLORA & FAUNA

THE MOST EXCITING PLANTS AND ANIMALS I SPOTTED ON MY TRIP

1.   3.

2.   4.

TAKE NOTHING BUT MEMORIES

MEMORABLE MOMENTS FROM MY TRIP

PARK RATING ☆ ☆ ☆ ☆ ☆   PLANNING A RETURN TRIP?   YES ☐ NO ☐

GREAT BASIN NATIONAL PARK

ESTABLISHED: 1986 • SIZE: 121 SQUARE MILES • LOCATION: EASTERN NEVADA
ANCESTRAL LAND OF THE WESTERN SHOSHONE, GOSHUTE, UTE, PAIUTE, AND WASHOE PEOPLES
FOR MORE INFORMATION: NPS.GOV/GRBA

From the 13,063-foot summit of Wheeler Peak to sage-covered foothills and Nevada's only remaining glacier (the southernmost glacier in the Northern Hemisphere!), Great Basin National Park is home to 800 species of plants and Nevada's largest and most spectacular cave system. Lehman Caves began forming around 2 to 5 million years ago, when the landscape was covered by warm, shallow ocean and limestone was formed by the shells of dead sea creatures accumulating on the ocean floor. Even after Lehman Caves was designated a national monument, the peaks and valleys surrounding the cave remained unprotected until the 1960s, when a group of biologists came to study the mysterious, 4,900-year-old bristlecone pine. Cave tours are offered frequently in peak season (June to September) and fall colors peak in early October. Be aware that the climate in the park varies drastically across the nearly 8,000-foot elevation change, no matter what the time of year.

The Bucket List Traveler Tip PLANNING TO HIKE WHEELER PEAK? SECURE A CAMPSITE AT WHEELER PEAK CAMPGROUND. IT'S A SHORT DRIVE TO THE TRAILHEAD FOR AN EARLY START TO ENSURE AMPLE TIME HIKING THE STRENUOUS TRAIL WHILE ENJOYING THE SCENERY. PACK YOUR WINDBREAKER—THE TRAIL IS EXPOSED ON THE RIDGELINE. SUPER WINDY!

ADVENTURE AWAITS!

DATE(S) VISITED:

TRAVEL COMPANION(S):

WEATHER:

LODGINGS:

NATIONAL PARK PASSPORT STAMP

NATIONAL PARK PASSPORT STAMP

ON THE TRAIL

MY FAVORITE WALKS, HIKES, AND VIEWS

1.

2.

3.

4.

FLORA & FAUNA

THE MOST EXCITING PLANTS AND ANIMALS I SPOTTED ON MY TRIP

1.

2.

3.

4.

TAKE NOTHING BUT MEMORIES

MEMORABLE MOMENTS FROM MY TRIP

PARK RATING ☆ ☆ ☆ ☆ ☆

PLANNING A RETURN TRIP?   YES ☐ NO ☐

GRAND CANYON NATIONAL PARK

ESTABLISHED: 1919 • SIZE: 1,902 SQUARE MILES • LOCATION: NORTHERN ARIZONA

ANCESTRAL LAND OF THE DINE (NAVAJO), HAVASUPAI, HUALAPAI, HOPI,

YAVAPAI-APACHE, KAIBAB, SOUTHERN PAIUTE, AND ZUNI PEOPLES

FOR MORE INFORMATION: NPS.GOV/GRCA

One of the seven natural wonders of the world that can be seen from space, Grand Canyon National Park encompasses 278 miles of the Colorado River and adjacent uplands. The mile-deep canyon's inner depths expose the Earth's history with rocks dating back 2 billion years. The first pioneers—prospectors looking to mine copper—began settling around the rim in the 1880s. They soon realized that tourism was more profitable than mining, which prompted the building of the Santa Fe Railroad to mobilize tourists from surrounding major cities. In 1903, President Roosevelt traveled to the Grand Canyon and declared portions of it a federal game reserve that later became a national monument, and, eventually, a national park. South Rim is open year-round, receiving about 90 percent of the park visitation, while the North Rim is open seasonally, from mid-May to mid-October.

The Bucket List Traveler Tip MY FAVORITE TIME TO EXPERIENCE THIS PARK IS DURING WINTER, WHEN HERMIT ROAD IS ACCESSIBLE BY PRIVATE VEHICLES. THAT PROVIDES FLEXIBILITY IN YOUR ITINERARY, BECAUSE YOU DON'T HAVE TO WAIT ON SHUTTLES. PLUS, ACCOMMODATIONS IN THE PARK ARE FAIRLY AFFORDABLE—AND AVAILABLE!

ADVENTURE AWAITS!

DATE(S) VISITED:
....

TRAVEL COMPANION(S):
....
....

WEATHER:
....

LODGINGS:
....

NATIONAL PARK PASSPORT STAMP

NATIONAL PARK PASSPORT STAMP

ON THE TRAIL

MY FAVORITE WALKS, HIKES, AND VIEWS

1.   3.

2.   4.

FLORA & FAUNA

THE MOST EXCITING PLANTS AND ANIMALS I SPOTTED ON MY TRIP

1.   3.

2.   4.

TAKE NOTHING BUT MEMORIES

MEMORABLE MOMENTS FROM MY TRIP

PARK RATING ☆ ☆ ☆ ☆ ☆   PLANNING A RETURN TRIP?   YES ☐ NO ☐

PETRIFIED FOREST NATIONAL PARK

ESTABLISHED: 1962 • SIZE: 346 SQUARE MILES • LOCATION: NORTHEASTERN ARIZONA
ANCESTRAL LAND OF THE ZUNI, PUEBLO, HOPI TUTSKWA, AND DINE BIKEYAH (NAVAJO) PEOPLES
FOR MORE INFORMATION: NPS.GOV/PEFO

Nature, geology, archaeology, paleontology, history, and sections of the "Mother Road": This intermountain basin high-desert park has it all. Rather than the traditional scenic alpine view of mountains and tree-lined vistas, this park boasts a forest—a *petrified* one. Petrified Forest National Park is a geologic treasure chest. Evidence of both Earth and human history exist here evidentially by fossils dating to 225 million years ago and Indigenous peoples' culture that dates back more than 13,000 years. You'll also find one of the most continuous sections of Triassic-age rocks ever discovered in the world, deposited here by enormous rivers. Something else not found at other national parks is the Museum Demonstration Lab, where you can chat with paleontologists at work and peek in the windows to view the fossils they're cleaning and conserving.

The Bucket List Traveler Tip BLUE MESA AND CRYSTAL FOREST ARE MY FAVORITE TRAILS. THE BRILLIANT COLORS IN THE PETRIFIED WOOD COME MAINLY FROM TRACE MINERALS. HERE'S A CHEAT SHEET: PURE QUARTZ IS WHITE; MANGANESE OXIDES FORM BLUE, PURPLE, BLACK, AND BROWN; AND IRON OXIDES PROVIDE HUES FROM YELLOW THROUGH RED TO BROWN AND BLACK.

ADVENTURE AWAITS!

DATE(S) VISITED:

TRAVEL COMPANION(S):

WEATHER:

LODGINGS:

NATIONAL PARK PASSPORT STAMP
NATIONAL PARK PASSPORT STAMP

ON THE TRAIL

MY FAVORITE WALKS, HIKES, AND VIEWS

1.   3.

2.   4.

FLORA & FAUNA

THE MOST EXCITING PLANTS AND ANIMALS I SPOTTED ON MY TRIP

1.   3.

2.   4.

TAKE NOTHING BUT MEMORIES

MEMORABLE MOMENTS FROM MY TRIP

PARK RATING ☆ ☆ ☆ ☆ ☆   **PLANNING A RETURN TRIP?**   YES ☐ NO ☐

SAGUARO NATIONAL PARK

ESTABLISHED: 1994 • SIZE: 143 SQUARE MILES • LOCATION: SOUTHERN ARIZONA
ANCESTRAL LAND OF THE AKIMEL O'ODHAM (PIMA), APACHE, HOPI, MARICOPA,
YAQUI, TOHONO O'ODHAM (DESERT PEOPLE), YAVAPAI, AND ZUNI PEOPLES
FOR MORE INFORMATION: NPS.GOV/SAGU

The saguaro cactus, native only to the Sonoran Desert in southern Arizona and northern Mexico, has the ability to store tons of water during rainy season. It only grows up to 1 inch during its first 13 years but will eventually reach 35 feet, with an average life span between 150 and 175 years. Saguaro National Park was established to protect this giant cactus and the desert, mountain, and riparian habitats within the associated Sonoran Desert and Sky Island. This land encompasses a wide range of elevations that support extraordinary biodiversity and preserves significant cultural resources and places important to Indigenous peoples. From cactus-covered desert to pine-cloaked mountain heights, the Saguaro Wilderness Area in the Rincon Mountains protects the last roadless mountain range in southern Arizona. The park has two districts geographically separated by the city of Tucson: the Rincon Mountain District (RMD), often referred to as Saguaro East, and the Tucson Mountain District (TMD), often referred to as Saguaro West.

The Bucket List Traveler Tip SHORT ON TIME? THE TWO SCENIC DRIVES (CACTUS FOREST DRIVE AND BAJADA LOOP DRIVE) ARE THE BEST WAY TO OPTIMIZE YOUR TIME AT THE PARK. YOU CAN DRIVE ALONG THE ROAD AND MAKE FREQUENT STOPS TO GET CLOSER TO THE CACTI.

ADVENTURE AWAITS!

DATE(S) VISITED:

TRAVEL COMPANION(S):

WEATHER:

LODGINGS:

NATIONAL PARK PASSPORT STAMP

NATIONAL PARK PASSPORT STAMP

ON THE TRAIL

MY FAVORITE WALKS, HIKES, AND VIEWS

1.   3.

2.   4.

FLORA & FAUNA

THE MOST EXCITING PLANTS AND ANIMALS I SPOTTED ON MY TRIP

1.   3.

2.   4.

TAKE NOTHING BUT MEMORIES

MEMORABLE MOMENTS FROM MY TRIP

PARK RATING ☆ ☆ ☆ ☆ ☆   **PLANNING A RETURN TRIP?**   YES ☐ NO ☐

HALEAKALĀ NATIONAL PARK

ESTABLISHED: 1961 • SIZE: 52 SQUARE MILES • LOCATION: EAST MAUI, HAWAI'I
ANCESTRAL LAND OF NATIVE HAWAIIANS AND POLYNESIANS FROM THE MARQUESAS ISLANDS
FOR MORE INFORMATION: NPS.GOV/HALE

Legend has it, it was here, on the giant shield volcano, that the demigod Maui snared the sun, releasing it only after it promised to move more slowly across the sky. Named after Haleakalā, a dormant volcano within its boundaries, this park extends from the 10,023-foot Summit District to the magnificent rainforest valley of Kīpahulu District near Hāna. Often misconstrued as a volcanic crater, Haleakalā Crater at the summit is a vast depression formed as erosion ate away a ridgeline, joining two valleys. Haleakalā National Park preserves the otherworldly volcanic landscape of the upper slopes of Haleakalā and protects the unique and fragile ecosystems of the Kīpahulu Valley. Striking plants and animals, such as Haleakalā silversword and nēnē, exist in this mountain region. In mid-March, the park hosts the Haleakalā Solar Festival, in conjunction with the National Solar Observatory, presenting mobile solar telescopes and hands-on solar science activities for all.

The Bucket List Traveler Tip WANT TO EXPERIENCE SUNRISE AT THE SUMMIT BUT DIDN'T BOOK A RESERVATION IN TIME? CONSIDER THE DOWNHILL BIKE TOUR WITH LOCAL CONCESSIONAIRES: YOU'LL BE TRANSPORTED TO THE SUMMIT FOR SUNRISE, THEN TRANSPORTED TO THE BASE OF THE PARK, WHERE YOU'LL BE LET LOOSE TO BIKE DOWNHILL BACK TO TOWN. BUCKET LIST, CHECK!

ADVENTURE AWAITS!

DATE(S) VISITED:

TRAVEL COMPANION(S):

WEATHER:

LODGINGS:

NATIONAL PARK PASSPORT STAMP

NATIONAL PARK PASSPORT STAMP

ON THE TRAIL

MY FAVORITE WALKS, HIKES, AND VIEWS

1.   3.

2.   4.

FLORA & FAUNA

THE MOST EXCITING PLANTS AND ANIMALS I SPOTTED ON MY TRIP

1.   3.

2.   4.

TAKE NOTHING BUT MEMORIES

MEMORABLE MOMENTS FROM MY TRIP

PARK RATING ☆ ☆ ☆ ☆ ☆   PLANNING A RETURN TRIP?   YES ☐   NO ☐

HAWAI'I VOLCANOES NATIONAL PARK

ESTABLISHED: 1916 • SIZE: 523 SQUARE MILES (AND COUNTING) • LOCATION: HAWAI'I ISLAND
ANCESTRAL LAND OF NATIVE HAWAIIANS AND POLYNESIANS FROM THE MARQUESAS ISLANDS
FOR MORE INFORMATION: NPS.GOV/HAVO

Given the nature of the island formed by a series of active volcanoes, new lands are constantly constructed here during lava flows. Hawai'i Volcanoes National Park extends from sea level to 13,681 feet, encompassing summits and rift zones of two of the world's most active volcanoes: Kīlauea and Mauna Loa. Mauna Loa is the largest active volcano on Earth, with more than 10,000 cubic miles of rock rising 30,000 feet from the bottom of the sea. Like all Hawaiian volcanoes, Mauna Loa is a shield volcano, characterized by broad and gently sloping sides that result from very fluid eruptions. The park preserves one of the largest significant ecosystems on the Hawaiian Islands, along with its cultural significance and historic sites. Every August, the Kīlauea Cultural Festival welcomes the public to enjoy hula performances, music, a variety of demonstrations such as traditional Hawaiian featherwork, and informational booths.

The Bucket List Traveler Tip FLY INTO HILO AND STAY IN TOWN IF YOU PLAN TO SPEND A LOT OF TIME EXPLORING THIS PARK. IT'S A QUICK 40-MINUTE DRIVE ONE WAY FROM THE PARK AND HILO IS A CHARMING TOWN AWAY FROM THE TOURIST TRAPS AND BIG RESORT CROWDS.

ADVENTURE AWAITS!

DATE(S) VISITED:

TRAVEL COMPANION(S):

WEATHER:

LODGINGS:

NATIONAL PARK PASSPORT STAMP
NATIONAL PARK PASSPORT STAMP

ON THE TRAIL

MY FAVORITE WALKS, HIKES, AND VIEWS

1.

2.

3.

4.

FLORA & FAUNA

THE MOST EXCITING PLANTS AND ANIMALS I SPOTTED ON MY TRIP

1.

2.

3.

4.

TAKE NOTHING BUT MEMORIES

MEMORABLE MOMENTS FROM MY TRIP

PARK RATING ☆ ☆ ☆ ☆ ☆

PLANNING A RETURN TRIP?   YES ☐ NO ☐

NATIONAL PARK OF AMERICAN SAMOA

ESTABLISHED: 1988 • SIZE: 21 SQUARE MILES • LOCATION: AMERICAN SAMOA
ANCESTRAL LAND OF THE INDIGENOUS SAMOANS OF POLYNESIAN ANCESTRY
FROM THE MARQUESAS ISLANDS
FOR MORE INFORMATION: NPS.GOV/NPSA

Talofa! (That means "Hello!" in Samoan.) National Park of American Samoa welcomes you to the only NPS site located south of the equator, which is also one of the most remote national parks in the country. Here, visitors get to experience largely undeveloped lands and waters across three islands: Tutuila, Ta'ū, and Ofu. The park preserves and protects the tropical rainforest, which is home to flying foxes, large fruit bats with 3-foot wingspans, coral reefs, and archaeological and cultural resources of American Samoa. The coral reef supports nearly 900 species of fish and a variety of birds, while 450 species of plants grow in the rainforest, approximately 30 percent of which are endemic to the archipelago. In keeping with the word *samoa*, meaning "sacred earth," the park helps protect fa'asamoa, the customs, beliefs, and traditions of the 3,000-year-old Samoan culture.

The Bucket List Traveler Tip SUNDAY IS THE DAY OF REST FOR SAMOANS—STORES ARE CLOSED, PUBLIC TRANSPORTATION IS NOT AVAILABLE, AND EVEN ACTIVITIES LIKE SWIMMING SHOULD BE AVOIDED. IF YOU WISH TO TAKE PHOTOS OF SOMEONE, CROSS THROUGH THEIR LAND, OR USE A VILLAGE BEACH, ALWAYS ASK PERMISSION FIRST. ALSO, WEAR MODEST SWIMWEAR TO RESPECT THE LOCAL CULTURE.

ADVENTURE AWAITS!

DATE(S) VISITED:

TRAVEL COMPANION(S):

WEATHER:

LODGINGS:

NATIONAL PARK PASSPORT STAMP

NATIONAL PARK PASSPORT STAMP

ON THE TRAIL

MY FAVORITE WALKS, HIKES, AND VIEWS

1.   3.

2.   4.

FLORA & FAUNA

THE MOST EXCITING PLANTS AND ANIMALS I SPOTTED ON MY TRIP

1.   3.

2.   4.

TAKE NOTHING BUT MEMORIES

MEMORABLE MOMENTS FROM MY TRIP

PARK RATING ☆ ☆ ☆ ☆ ☆   PLANNING A RETURN TRIP?   YES ☐ NO ☐

ROCKY MOUNTAIN

Perhaps unsurprisingly, this is where you'll find many of the tallest, longest, and largest features of our national parks, ranging from wonders crafted by Mother Nature to human-made structures both above- and underground. Impressive features of this region include one of the highest national parks in the nation, with elevations from 7,860 feet to 14,259 feet; the two tallest dunes in North America; the largest high-altitude lake in North America; the highest concentration of natural sandstone arches in the world; and the tallest cliff in Colorado, which also comes third in the continental United States after El Capitan and Notch Peak, exposing some of the world's oldest rock. As far as wildlife goes, this is where you'll find one of the largest remaining grizzly bear populations in the Lower 48 and one of the world's richest fossil beds from the late Eocene and Oligocene epochs. This is also where the world's first national park was established. Included in this section are the national parks located in Montana, Wyoming, Utah, Colorado, and North and South Dakota.

Montana
- [ ] GLACIER NATIONAL PARK

Wyoming
- [ ] YELLOWSTONE NATIONAL PARK
- [ ] GRAND TETON NATIONAL PARK

Utah
- [ ] ZION NATIONAL PARK
- [ ] BRYCE CANYON NATIONAL PARK
- [ ] CAPITOL REEF NATIONAL PARK
- [ ] CANYONLANDS NATIONAL PARK
- [ ] ARCHES NATIONAL PARK

Colorado
- [ ] MESA VERDE NATIONAL PARK
- [ ] BLACK CANYON OF THE GUNNISON NATIONAL PARK
- [ ] ROCKY MOUNTAIN NATIONAL PARK
- [ ] GREAT SAND DUNES NATIONAL PARK

North Dakota
- [ ] THEODORE ROOSEVELT NATIONAL PARK

South Dakota
- [ ] WIND CAVE NATIONAL PARK
- [ ] BADLANDS NATIONAL PARK

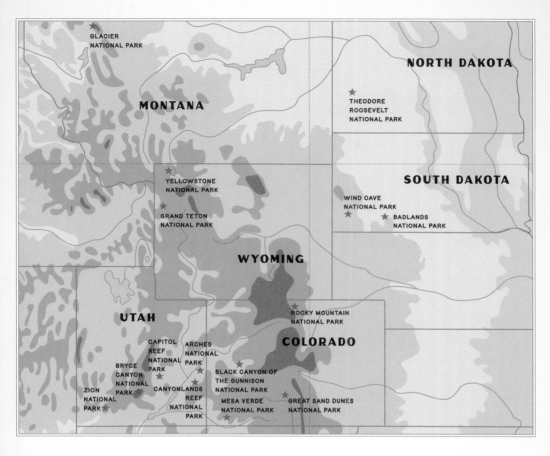

GLACIER
NATIONAL PARK

NORTH DAKOTA

MONTANA

THEODORE
ROOSEVELT
NATIONAL PARK

SOUTH DAKOTA

YELLOWSTONE
NATIONAL PARK

WIND CAVE
NATIONAL PARK

BADLANDS
NATIONAL PARK

GRAND TETON
NATIONAL PARK

WYOMING

UTAH

ROCKY MOUNTAIN
NATIONAL PARK

CAPITOL
REEF
NATIONAL
PARK

ARCHES
NATIONAL
PARK

COLORADO

BRYCE
CANYON
NATIONAL
PARK

BLACK CANYON OF
THE GUNNISON
NATIONAL PARK

ZION
NATIONAL
PARK

CANYONLANDS
REEF
NATIONAL
PARK

MESA VERDE
NATIONAL PARK

GREAT SAND DUNES
NATIONAL PARK

GLACIER NATIONAL PARK

ESTABLISHED: 1910 • SIZE: 1,583 SQUARE MILES • LOCATION: NORTHWESTERN MONTANA
ANCESTRAL LAND OF THE BLACKFEET, SALISH, PEND D'OREILLE, AND KOOTENAI PEOPLES
FOR MORE INFORMATION: NPS.GOV/GLAC

Home to a rare hydrologic feature, the Triple Divide Peak, Glacier National Park is the Crown of the Continent. It straddles the Continental Divide, which separates the Atlantic and Pacific watersheds of North America. Named for remnants of glaciers from the ice ages, this park contains 25 glaciers that are actively thawing and melting. The largest glacier in the park, Blackfoot Glacier, is merely 0.7 square mile. In addition to protecting the last remaining glacier from the Little Ice Age within this region, the park preserves 1 million acres of glacier-carved peaks and valleys, pristine turquoise lakes and streams, wildflower fields during the warm summer months, dense ancient forests that provide habitat to 71 species of mammals, abundant wildlife, exceptionally long geologic history and natural processes, and rich cultural heritage. A notable annual summer event is Native America Speaks, in which tribal members share personal knowledge of their history and culture through singing, storytelling, presentations, and hands-on learning.

The Bucket List Traveler Tip IF YOU HAVE YET TO VISIT GLACIER NATIONAL PARK, GO BEFORE WE LOSE ITS NAMESAKE. SOME SPOTS TO VIEW THEM: JACKSON GLACIER FROM GOING-TO-THE-SUN ROAD OVERLOOK, SALAMANDER GLACIER WHEN DRIVING INTO MANY GLACIER, SPERRY GLACIER FROM HIDDEN LAKE OVERLOOK, PIEGAN GLACIER FROM PRESTON PARK, GRINNELL GLACIER TRAIL, AND SEXTON GLACIER FROM SIYEH PASS TRAIL.

ADVENTURE AWAITS!

DATE(S) VISITED:

TRAVEL COMPANION(S):

WEATHER:

LODGINGS:

NATIONAL PARK PASSPORT STAMP

NATIONAL PARK PASSPORT STAMP

ON THE TRAIL

MY FAVORITE WALKS, HIKES, AND VIEWS

1.   3.

2.   4.

FLORA & FAUNA

THE MOST EXCITING PLANTS AND ANIMALS I SPOTTED ON MY TRIP

1.   3.

2.   4.

TAKE NOTHING BUT MEMORIES

MEMORABLE MOMENTS FROM MY TRIP

PARK RATING ☆ ☆ ☆ ☆ ☆   PLANNING A RETURN TRIP?   YES ☐   NO ☐

YELLOWSTONE NATIONAL PARK

ESTABLISHED: 1872 • SIZE: 3,471 SQUARE MILES • LOCATION: NORTHWESTERN WYOMING
ANCESTRAL LAND OF THE SHOSHONE, KIOWA, CROW, BLACKFEET, CAYUSE,
COEUR D'ALENE, NEZ PERCE, FLATHEAD, AND LAKOTA PEOPLES
FOR MORE INFORMATION: NPS.GOV/YELL

Known today as Yellowstone National Park, this region contains traces of human exploration and occupation dating back at least 12,000 years. Sitting on top of a dormant volcano where 50 percent of the world's hydrothermal features are located, Yellowstone is home to one of the world's largest calderas, 10,000 thermal features, more than 300 geysers, one of the world's largest petrified forests, and more than 290 waterfalls. It's hard to imagine or believe the landscape without personally seeing the colorful hot springs, boiling mud pots, billowing clouds of fumaroles steam, travertine terraces, the park's very own Grand Canyon, and the wide-open valleys where the oldest and largest public herd of bison in the country freely roam. The best months to visit are April and September-October, when bears emerge from hibernation. Migrating birds arrive just before May and elk rut begins mid-September.

The Bucket List Traveler Tip DON'T PET THE FLUFFY COWS! STAY AT LEAST 25 YARDS FROM BISON AND ELK AND 100 YARDS FROM BEARS AND WOLVES. DON'T STOP IN THE MIDDLE OF THE ROAD OR OBSTRUCT TRAFFIC WHEN SPOTTING WILDLIFE (IT'S DANGEROUS AND INCONSIDERATE). AND STAY ON DESIGNATED TRAILS AND BOARDWALKS.

ADVENTURE AWAITS!

DATE(S) VISITED:

TRAVEL COMPANION(S):

WEATHER:

LODGINGS:

NATIONAL PARK PASSPORT STAMP

NATIONAL PARK PASSPORT STAMP

ON THE TRAIL

MY FAVORITE WALKS, HIKES, AND VIEWS

1.

2.

3.

4.

FLORA & FAUNA

THE MOST EXCITING PLANTS AND ANIMALS I SPOTTED ON MY TRIP

1.

2.

3.

4.

TAKE NOTHING BUT MEMORIES

MEMORABLE MOMENTS FROM MY TRIP

PARK RATING ☆ ☆ ☆ ☆ ☆

PLANNING A
RETURN TRIP?

YES ☐ NO ☐

GRAND TETON NATIONAL PARK

ESTABLISHED: 1929 • SIZE: 485 SQUARE MILES • LOCATION: NORTHWESTERN WYOMING

ANCESTRAL LAND OF THE SHOSHONE, BANNOCK, BLACKFOOT, CROW,

FLATHEAD, GROS VENTRE, AND NEZ PERCE PEOPLES

FOR MORE INFORMATION: NPS.GOV/GRTE

Home to some of the oldest rocks in the national park system dating nearly 2.7 billion years ago, Grand Teton National Park protects the lush valley floors, mountain meadows, alpine lakes, and rising peaks of the Teton mountain range from commercial exploitation. Local ranchers and businesspeople wanted to preserve the valley and eliminate unwanted development of the open spaces, and then John D. Rockefeller Jr. purchased private lands later to be donated to the federal government. Animosity toward expanding governmental control and a perceived loss of individual freedoms fueled anti-park sentiments that nearly derailed establishment of the park. Though winter shuts down many amenities and roads nowadays, it's a great time to experience the region by snowshoe, cross-country skis, or snowmobile.

The Bucket List Traveler Tip THE PARK IS BLACK AND GRIZZLY BEAR COUNTRY. REMEMBER THREE THINGS WHEN HIKING: CARRY BEAR SPRAY, KNOW HOW TO USE IT, AND MAKE SURE IT'S EASILY ACCESSIBLE; HIKE IN PAIRS OR WITH GROUPS, LIKE A GUIDED HIKE WITH A PARK RANGER; AND BE NOISY SO BEARS ARE AWARE OF YOUR PRESENCE AND AVOID YOU.

ADVENTURE AWAITS!

DATE(S) VISITED:

TRAVEL COMPANION(S):

WEATHER:

LODGINGS:

NATIONAL PARK PASSPORT STAMP

NATIONAL PARK PASSPORT STAMP

ON THE TRAIL

MY FAVORITE WALKS, HIKES, AND VIEWS

1.   3.

2.   4.

FLORA & FAUNA

THE MOST EXCITING PLANTS AND ANIMALS I SPOTTED ON MY TRIP

1.   3.

2.   4.

TAKE NOTHING BUT MEMORIES

MEMORABLE MOMENTS FROM MY TRIP

PARK RATING ☆ ☆ ☆ ☆ ☆   **PLANNING A RETURN TRIP?**   YES ☐ NO ☐

ZION NATIONAL PARK

ESTABLISHED: 1919 (1909) • SIZE: 229 SQUARE MILES • LOCATION: SOUTHWESTERN UTAH
ANCESTRAL LAND OF THE PUEBLO AND SOUTHERN PAIUTE PEOPLES
FOR MORE INFORMATION: NPS.GOV/ZION

Zion was the first national park established in Utah. Initially created as Mukuntuweap National Monument, the park is home to a variety of wildlife, hardy desert plants, and rare and threatened birds. It's known for its many features: expansive canyon walls carved by the Virgin River, lush hanging gardens, scenic vistas, and historic rock art. People have inhabited this landscape for more than 10,000 years, and the park's prehistoric art and artifacts tell the stories of Indigenous peoples, European and American fur trappers, government surveyors, and pioneers from the Church of Jesus Christ of Latter-Day Saints. Weather in Zion varies greatly from hot summers to mild winters that may bring trail-closing snow. The annual Zion Canyon Music Festival in Springdale is on the last weekend of September, so plan for it or avoid visiting during that time.

The Bucket List Traveler Tip THE BEST TIMES TO VISIT ZION ARE LATE MARCH AND LATE NOVEMBER. SHUTTLE LINES AND WAIT TIMES ARE BEARABLE COMPARED TO SUMMER AND TEMPERATURES ARE ALSO A LOT MILDER. I'VE DRIVEN INTO ZION CANYON WHEN SHUTTLES WEREN'T OPERATING, BUT IT'S STILL MORE CONVENIENT TO TAKE THE SHUTTLE INTO THE CANYON BECAUSE PARKING SITUATIONS ARE QUITE HORRENDOUS.

ADVENTURE AWAITS!

DATE(S) VISITED:

TRAVEL COMPANION(S):

WEATHER:

LODGINGS:

NATIONAL PARK PASSPORT STAMP

NATIONAL PARK PASSPORT STAMP

ON THE TRAIL

MY FAVORITE WALKS, HIKES, AND VIEWS

1.   3.

2.   4.

FLORA & FAUNA

THE MOST EXCITING PLANTS AND ANIMALS I SPOTTED ON MY TRIP

1.   3.

2.   4.

TAKE NOTHING BUT MEMORIES

MEMORABLE MOMENTS FROM MY TRIP

PARK RATING ☆ ☆ ☆ ☆ ☆   PLANNING A
                               RETURN TRIP?   YES ☐ NO ☐

BRYCE CANYON NATIONAL PARK

ESTABLISHED: 1928 (1923) • SIZE: 56 SQUARE MILES • LOCATION: SOUTHERN UTAH
ANCESTRAL LAND OF THE SOUTHERN PAIUTE, HOPI, ZUNI, UTE, PUEBLO, AND NAVAJO PEOPLES
FOR MORE INFORMATION: NPS.GOV/BRCA

Technically, Bryce Canyon is not a canyon, but instead a series of 14 massive bowl-shaped amphitheaters sculpted by drainage of seasonal rains and melting snow. The Paunsaugunt Plateau was first used for seasonal hunting and gathering activities by the Paiute people. Later explored by a government surveyor and pioneer named Ebenezer Bryce in the late 1800s, the area became known as "Bryce's Canyon." Interest in the canyon peaked as the remote area became more accessible when Union Pacific expanded rail service. Bryce Canyon was established soon after to preserve the ethereal landscape consisting of domes, pinnacles, and hoodoos. The Southern Paiute people believe that these strange "red-painted faces" hoodoos were the "evil legend people" who were cursed into stone by the powerful Coyote spirit. The park hosts several events throughout the year, with two of note: the Astronomy Festival in June for this International Dark Sky Park and the Bryce Canyon Geology Festival in summertime.

The Bucket List Traveler Tip YOU CAN DO AND SEE A LOT HERE IN A DAY. CATCH SUNRISE BETWEEN SUNSET AND SUNRISE POINTS, HIKE DOWN THE WALL STREET SECTION OF NAVAJO LOOP, AND HIKE THROUGH THE HOODOOS BEFORE HEADING BACK UP VIA QUEENS GARDEN TRAIL. THEN DRIVE THE SOUTHERN SCENIC DRIVE TO RAINBOW POINT. HEAD BACK NORTH AND STOP AT THE VISITOR CENTER BEFORE GOING BACK TO THE RIM FOR SUNSET AT THE PARIA VIEW.

ADVENTURE AWAITS!

DATE(S) VISITED:

TRAVEL COMPANION(S):

WEATHER:

LODGINGS:

NATIONAL PARK PASSPORT STAMP

NATIONAL PARK PASSPORT STAMP

ON THE TRAIL

MY FAVORITE WALKS, HIKES, AND VIEWS

1.

2.

3.

4.

FLORA & FAUNA

THE MOST EXCITING PLANTS AND ANIMALS I SPOTTED ON MY TRIP

1.

2.

3.

4.

TAKE NOTHING BUT MEMORIES

MEMORABLE MOMENTS FROM MY TRIP

PARK RATING ☆ ☆ ☆ ☆ ☆

PLANNING A
RETURN TRIP?

YES ☐ NO ☐

CAPITOL REEF NATIONAL PARK

ESTABLISHED: 1971 (1937) • SIZE: 378 SQUARE MILES • LOCATION: SOUTHERN UTAH

ANCESTRAL LAND OF THE UTE, PAIUTE, NAVAJO, HOPI, ZUNI, AND PUEBLO PEOPLES

FOR MORE INFORMATION: NPS.GOV/CARE

Capitol Reef National Park is an oasis of colorful sandstone, home to the nearly 100-mile-long Waterpocket Fold—a massive geological outcrop that emerged during a series of mountain-building events 70 million years ago. The park was named "Capitol" for the monolithic white domes of Navajo Sandstone that resemble the top of the US Capitol building, and "Reef" for the rocky cliffs that act as a barrier to travel, like an underwater ocean reef. Spring and fall are optimal times to visit, for mild temperatures and crowds, though as temperatures decline in September, crowds pick back up during apple harvest season and when the cottonwood trees start changing colors.

The Bucket List Traveler Tip SLOW YOUR PACE AND SAVOR THE MOMENT. STOP BY THE FRUITA HISTORIC DISTRICT TO PICK FRUITS FROM ITS ORCHARDS OR SIT FOR SOME PIES FROM THE GIFFORD HOUSE STORE. FIND PEACE AND SOLITUDE AS YOU WANDER THE TRAILS OR OVER TO THE OTHER SIDE OF WATERPOCKET FOLD AT THE TWO EASTERN DISTRICTS.

ADVENTURE AWAITS!

DATE(S) VISITED:

TRAVEL COMPANION(S):

WEATHER:

LODGINGS:

NATIONAL PARK PASSPORT STAMP

NATIONAL PARK PASSPORT STAMP

ON THE TRAIL

MY FAVORITE WALKS, HIKES, AND VIEWS

1.   3.

2.   4.

FLORA & FAUNA

THE MOST EXCITING PLANTS AND ANIMALS I SPOTTED ON MY TRIP

1.   3.

2.   4.

TAKE NOTHING BUT MEMORIES

MEMORABLE MOMENTS FROM MY TRIP

PARK RATING ☆ ☆ ☆ ☆ ☆

PLANNING A RETURN TRIP?

YES ☐ NO ☐

CANYONLANDS NATIONAL PARK

ESTABLISHED: 1964 • SIZE: 527 SQUARE MILES • LOCATION: SOUTHEASTERN UTAH
ANCESTRAL LAND OF THE UTE, SOUTHERN PAIUTE, PUEBLO, AND NAVAJO PEOPLES
FOR MORE INFORMATION: NPS.GOV/CANY

Canyonlands preserves an immense and colorful landscape that has eroded into countless canyons, mesas, arches, fins, spires, and buttes sculpted by the Green and Colorado Rivers. Water and gravity are the prime architects of this carefully curated landscape, cutting flat layers of sedimentary rock into the features we see today. With the growth of the country's nuclear arms program in the 1950s, the Atomic Energy Commission offered monetary incentives to discover and deliver uranium ore. Prospectors built numerous exploratory roads in this area, in search of "radioactive gold." Canyonlands was created to protect the area from these uranium mining activities. These roads still exist today for four-wheeling, and as the scars are slowly revegetating, the landscape is returning to its natural state. The park is divided into three major districts— Island in the Sky, the Needles, and the Maze—and traveling between them requires 2 to 6 hours by car.

The Bucket List Traveler Tip A TRIP TO CANYONLANDS SHOULD BE COMBINED WITH ARCHES NATIONAL PARK (AND DEAD HORSE POINT STATE PARK). IF TIME PERMITS, ADD A TRIP TO NATURAL BRIDGES NATIONAL MONUMENT, MONUMENT VALLEY TRIBAL PARK (DON'T MISS THE FAMOUS *FORREST GUMP* SPOT BY THE ROADSIDE), HOVENWEEP NATIONAL MONUMENT, AND MESA VERDE NATIONAL PARK.

ADVENTURE AWAITS!

DATE(S) VISITED:

TRAVEL COMPANION(S):

WEATHER:

LODGINGS:

NATIONAL PARK PASSPORT STAMP

NATIONAL PARK PASSPORT STAMP

ON THE TRAIL

MY FAVORITE WALKS, HIKES, AND VIEWS

1.   3.

2.   4.

FLORA & FAUNA

THE MOST EXCITING PLANTS AND ANIMALS I SPOTTED ON MY TRIP

1.   3.

2.   4.

TAKE NOTHING BUT MEMORIES

MEMORABLE MOMENTS FROM MY TRIP

PARK RATING ☆ ☆ ☆ ☆ ☆   PLANNING A RETURN TRIP?   YES ☐ NO ☐

ARCHES NATIONAL PARK

ESTABLISHED: 1971 (1929) • SIZE: 119 SQUARE MILES • LOCATION: SOUTHEASTERN UTAH
ANCESTRAL LAND OF THE SOUTHERN UTE, SOUTHERN PAIUTE, HOPI, PUEBLO, AND NAVAJO PEOPLES
FOR MORE INFORMATION: NPS.GOV/ARCH

Towering sandstone fins and weathered arches make this park a treasure trove of geological wonders. Appropriately named Arches National Park boasts the largest concentration of natural sandstone arches on Earth. With more than 2,000 arches scattered across the park, there are several rockstars that live here: Landscape Arch is the longest span of any arch in North America at 306 feet; the southern span of Double Arch soars 112 feet aboveground, making it the tallest opening for a natural arch; and the most famous is the largest freestanding arch in the park, the Delicate Arch. The park was initially established by securing acreage in Devils Garden to promote tourism, though the boundaries have expanded since. April, May, September, and October typically see daytime temperatures ranging from 70°F to 80°F, making it the most comfortable time of year to visit and attracting crowds outside summer and holidays. The third weekend in October is also busy, when Utah public schools typically have a fall break.

The Bucket List Traveler Tip TO MINIMIZE WAIT TIME, ENTER THE PARK BEFORE 8 A.M. OR AFTER 5 P.M. ARCHES IS LESS CROWDED AT SUNRISE AND SUNSET, AND THOSE ARE ALSO THE MOST STRIKING TIMES TO VISIT FOR PHOTOGRAPHY AND LIGHTING. HEAD TO BED EARLY AND ENTER THE PARK BEFORE 7 A.M. TO SKIP THE TICKETED TIMED-ENTRY PROCESS.

ADVENTURE AWAITS!

DATE(S) VISITED:

TRAVEL COMPANION(S):

WEATHER:

LODGINGS:

NATIONAL PARK PASSPORT STAMP

NATIONAL PARK PASSPORT STAMP

ON THE TRAIL

MY FAVORITE WALKS, HIKES, AND VIEWS

1.   3.

2.   4.

FLORA & FAUNA

THE MOST EXCITING PLANTS AND ANIMALS I SPOTTED ON MY TRIP

1.   3.

2.   4.

TAKE NOTHING BUT MEMORIES

MEMORABLE MOMENTS FROM MY TRIP

PARK RATING ☆ ☆ ☆ ☆ ☆   PLANNING A RETURN TRIP?   YES ☐ NO ☐

MESA VERDE NATIONAL PARK

ESTABLISHED: 1906 • SIZE: 81 SQUARE MILES • LOCATION: SOUTHWEST COLORADO
ANCESTRAL LAND OF THE PUEBLO PEOPLE
FOR MORE INFORMATION: NPS.GOV/MEVE

The first archaeological area in the world to be recognized and protected by the federal government, Mesa Verde National Park is home to the Ancestral Puebloans, who shifted their dwelling sites from mesa tops into sheltered alcoves in canyon walls. They began to build cliff houses, where the air is thin and the views are spectacular. There are approximately 600 cliff dwellings in the park, making it rich in history. The largest cliff dwelling, Cliff Palace, housed as many as 250 people in its 217 rooms and 23 kivas. The second-largest cliff dwelling, Long House, has 150 rooms and 21 kivas where 150 people lived. The park was named a UNESCO World Heritage Site in recognition of its exceptional archaeological history. The road into the park is a narrow, steep mountain road starting at 6,900 feet and rising to 8,570 feet. The first view of a cliff dwelling is 21 miles past the park entrance.

The Bucket List Traveler Tip

THE PARK IS TUCKED AWAY IN THE SOUTHWEST CORNER OF COLORADO, SO MAKE THE MOST OF YOUR TRIP BY EXTENDING IT A DAY OR TWO AND STOPPING BY THE FOUR CORNERS MONUMENT NAVAJO TRIBAL PARK (AN HOUR DRIVE). CHECK OFF THE BUCKET LIST BEING IN FOUR STATES AT THE SAME TIME!

ADVENTURE AWAITS!

DATE(S) VISITED:

TRAVEL COMPANION(S):

WEATHER:

LODGINGS:

NATIONAL PARK PASSPORT STAMP

NATIONAL PARK PASSPORT STAMP

ON THE TRAIL

MY FAVORITE WALKS, HIKES, AND VIEWS

1.   3.

2.   4.

FLORA & FAUNA

THE MOST EXCITING PLANTS AND ANIMALS I SPOTTED ON MY TRIP

1.   3.

2.   4.

TAKE NOTHING BUT MEMORIES

MEMORABLE MOMENTS FROM MY TRIP

PARK RATING ☆ ☆ ☆ ☆ ☆

PLANNING A RETURN TRIP?   YES ☐ NO ☐

BLACK CANYON OF THE GUNNISON NATIONAL PARK

ESTABLISHED: 1999 (1933) • SIZE: 47 SQUARE MILES • LOCATION: WESTERN COLORADO
ANCESTRAL LAND OF THE UTE PEOPLE
FOR MORE INFORMATION: NPS.GOV/BLCA

Often referred to as "Colorado's own Grand Canyon," Black Canyon of the Gunnison comprises 14 of the deepest and most dramatic sections of the 48-mile-long canyon. Some canyons are steep, deep, or narrow, but Black Canyon combines all three, evidenced by the river dropping an average of 96 feet per mile. The park was first created to protect from future development due to citizens' concern upon the completion of a road to the rim of the canyon, thereby making it accessible. Today, Black Canyon of the Gunnison preserves some of the world's oldest exposed rock from the Precambrian era roughly 2 billion years ago, the Gunnison River carving through solid metamorphic rock, and the space to recreate in solitude. The park's high elevation and low humidity is perfect in spring, when all roads and trails are open after winter closure.

The Bucket List Traveler Tip DRAGON POINT OVERLOOK IS PERFECT FOR SUNSETS. SUNRISE LOVER? WITNESS THE STUNNING PINK AND ORANGE LIGHT SLOWLY SHINE ACROSS THE PAINTED WALL AT CHASM VIEW (NORTH RIM). OTHER PICTURESQUE OVERLOOKS ARE GUNNISON POINT AND SUNSET VIEW. HIKE THE NORTH VISTA TRAIL TO THE EXCLAMATION POINT SIGN FOR A VIEW THAT'LL MAKE YOU . . . !!!

ADVENTURE AWAITS!

DATE(S) VISITED:

TRAVEL COMPANION(S):

WEATHER:

LODGINGS:

NATIONAL PARK   PASSPORT STAMP

NATIONAL PARK   PASSPORT STAMP

ON THE TRAIL

MY FAVORITE WALKS, HIKES, AND VIEWS

1.   3.

2.   4.

FLORA & FAUNA

THE MOST EXCITING PLANTS AND ANIMALS I SPOTTED ON MY TRIP

1.   3.

2.   4.

TAKE NOTHING BUT MEMORIES

MEMORABLE MOMENTS FROM MY TRIP

PARK RATING ☆ ☆ ☆ ☆ ☆   PLANNING A
RETURN TRIP?   YES ☐ NO ☐

ROCKY MOUNTAIN NATIONAL PARK

ESTABLISHED: 1915 • SIZE: 415 SQUARE MILES • LOCATION: NORTHERN COLORADO
ANCESTRAL LAND OF THE UTE AND ARAPAHO PEOPLES
FOR MORE INFORMATION: NPS.GOV/ROMO

Rugged postcard-perfect peaks, glistening lakes, land above the trees, and jaw-dropping beauty on top of the world: Rocky Mountain National Park is home to more than 70 peaks rising above 12,000 feet, 147 lakes, 7 glaciers, and 70 species of mammals (including more than 3,000 elk, 400 bighorn sheep, and numerous mule deer and moose). Many of the taller peaks make up the Continental Divide, where snowmelt runs either west to the Pacific Ocean or east to the Atlantic. The park supports and protects three ecosystems, montane, subalpine, and alpine tundra, which makes up one-third of the park's area. More than 700 species of plant life can be found here, so it's clear why Rocky Mountain National Park deserves its status as a UNESCO World Biosphere Reserve. Wildflower lovers should visit in June and July, when meadows and hillsides are splashed with botanical color. Enjoy golden aspens and the rowdy antics of elk rut during mating season in autumn and snowscapes and solitude in winter.

The Bucket List Traveler Tip IF YOU'RE UNABLE TO SECURE AN ENTRY PERMIT IN ADVANCE, TRY AGAIN EXACTLY 24 HOURS BEFORE YOUR PLANNED ENTRY TIME, AS 40 PERCENT OF THE PERMITS ARE RELEASED AT THAT TIME. ANOTHER OPTION IS TO SHOW UP BEFORE 9 A.M. OR AFTER 2 P.M., WHEN NO PERMIT IS NEEDED.

ADVENTURE AWAITS!

DATE(S) VISITED:

TRAVEL COMPANION(S):

NATIONAL PARK PASSPORT STAMP

NATIONAL PARK PASSPORT STAMP

WEATHER:

LODGINGS:

ON THE TRAIL

MY FAVORITE WALKS, HIKES, AND VIEWS

1.   3.

2.   4.

FLORA & FAUNA

THE MOST EXCITING PLANTS AND ANIMALS I SPOTTED ON MY TRIP

1.   3.

2.   4.

TAKE NOTHING BUT MEMORIES

MEMORABLE MOMENTS FROM MY TRIP

PARK RATING ☆ ☆ ☆ ☆ ☆   PLANNING A
RETURN TRIP?   YES ☐ NO ☐

GREAT SAND DUNES NATIONAL PARK

ESTABLISHED: 2007 (1932) • SIZE: 167 SQUARE MILES • LOCATION: SOUTHERN COLORADO
ANCESTRAL LAND OF THE UTE, CHEYENNE, APACHE, NAVAJO, AND PUEBLO PEOPLES
FOR MORE INFORMATION: NPS.GOV/GRSA

Great Sand Dunes National Park preserves strikingly unique sand dunes and the surrounding environment of alpine tundra, subalpine forest, montane woodlands, and riparian zones, along with their high-elevation watersheds. The Great Sand Dunes are believed to have originated from large lakes that once covered portions of the San Luis Valley around 440,000 years ago. The lakes dried up and the dunefield emerged at the base of the Sangre de Cristo Mountains. Star Dune, the star of the sandbox, is the tallest dune in the North America continent, measuring 750 feet. The iconic sandhill cranes spend part of their spring and fall in the San Luis Valley, arriving in early February to build up energy by feasting on barley grains. By late March, they head north to raise their young, then return in late September.

The Bucket List Traveler Tip MEDANO CREEK USUALLY ARRIVES AT THE DUNES PARKING AREA SOMETIME IN APRIL, WITH PEAK FLOW IN LATE MAY AND EARLY JUNE. BRING YOUR INNER TUBES FOR THE CREEK AND YOUR SANDBOARD OR SLED FOR THE DUNE SLOPES. MOSQUITOES EMERGE IN LARGE NUMBERS BY MID-JUNE, SO PLAN ACCORDINGLY AND PACK YOUR BUG SPRAY.

ADVENTURE AWAITS!

DATE(S) VISITED:

TRAVEL COMPANION(S):

WEATHER:

LODGINGS:

NATIONAL PARK PASSPORT STAMP

NATIONAL PARK PASSPORT STAMP

ON THE TRAIL

MY FAVORITE WALKS, HIKES, AND VIEWS

1.   3.

2.   4.

FLORA & FAUNA

THE MOST EXCITING PLANTS AND ANIMALS I SPOTTED ON MY TRIP

1.   3.

2.   4.

TAKE NOTHING BUT MEMORIES

MEMORABLE MOMENTS FROM MY TRIP

PARK RATING ☆ ☆ ☆ ☆ ☆   PLANNING A RETURN TRIP?   YES ☐   NO ☐

THEODORE ROOSEVELT NATIONAL PARK

ESTABLISHED: 1978 (1947) • SIZE: 110 SQUARE MILES • LOCATION: WESTERN NORTH DAKOTA
ANCESTRAL LAND OF THE MANDAN, HIDATSA, AND ARIKARA PEOPLES
FOR MORE INFORMATION: NPS.GOV/THRO

Theodore Roosevelt National Park preserves the land that its namesake president loved. His time spent here hunting bison inspired him to go down the path of conservation advocacy and policy. This piece of land forever impacted the United States by way of creation of our national parks—and the removal of Indigenous peoples from their ancestral lands. A national park like this is a tremendous resource, home to elk, prairie dogs, and more than 500 bison that once disappeared from the area in the late 1800s. Its beautifully bizarre multifaceted land includes the living heritage of its first people and the emergence of the man it's named for. For ideal conditions, visit in late spring or early fall, when temperatures are pleasant.

The Bucket List Traveler Tip DON'T SKIP THE NORTH UNIT OF THE PARK. THE SOUTH UNIT GETS MORE VISITATION DUE TO ITS PROXIMITY TO THE FREEWAY, BUT THE NORTH UNIT IS WHERE THINGS GET INTERESTING IN TERMS OF GEOLOGY, SCENIC VISTAS, LONGHORN CATTLE, AND A LOT FEWER PEOPLE.

ADVENTURE AWAITS!

DATE(S) VISITED:
....

TRAVEL COMPANION(S):
....

....

WEATHER:
....

LODGINGS:
....

NATIONAL PARK PASSPORT STAMP

NATIONAL PARK PASSPORT STAMP

ON THE TRAIL

MY FAVORITE WALKS, HIKES, AND VIEWS

1.

2.

3.

4.

FLORA & FAUNA

THE MOST EXCITING PLANTS AND ANIMALS I SPOTTED ON MY TRIP

1.

2.

3.

4.

TAKE NOTHING BUT MEMORIES

MEMORABLE MOMENTS FROM MY TRIP

....

....

....

....

....

....

....

....

....

....

....

....

PARK RATING ☆ ☆ ☆ ☆ ☆

PLANNING A RETURN TRIP? YES ☐ NO ☐

WIND CAVE NATIONAL PARK

ESTABLISHED: 1903 • SIZE: 44 SQUARE MILES • LOCATION: SOUTHWESTERN SOUTH DAKOTA
ANCESTRAL LAND OF THE LAKOTA AND CHEYENNE PEOPLES
FOR MORE INFORMATION: NPS.GOV/WICA

Featuring rolling hills, mixed-grass prairies, and quintessential boxwork formations in a cave where the Lakota Nation emerged, Wind Cave protects two very different worlds above- and underground. It's the first cave that garnered national park designation, featuring the world's largest concentration of rare boxwork formations. The park is home to the third longest cave in the United States—after Mammoth Cave and Jewel Cave—with more than 160 miles of explored passageways. Wind Cave is a limestone cavern deposited by a great inland sea more than 300 million years ago. The limestone, subjected to several periods of uplift, fractured in all directions at all angles. Boxwork, made of thin calcite blades projecting from cave walls and ceilings forming a honeycomb pattern, was then formed when dissolved calcium carbonate crystallized within the fractures. Though the cave itself is 54°F year-round, temperatures aboveground vary with the seasons, as always.

The Bucket List Traveler Tip ALL TOUR OPTIONS SHOWCASE THE RARE BOXWORK FORMATIONS. YOUR TOUR SELECTION DEPENDS ON ANY TIME AND/OR PHYSICAL CONSTRAINTS YOU HAVE. I WENT ON THE NATURAL ENTRANCE AND FAIRGROUNDS TOURS. IF YOU ONLY HAVE TIME AND FUNDS FOR ONE TOUR, FAIRGROUNDS TOUR IS A GREAT SELECTION THAT COVERS A LOT OF GROUND.

ADVENTURE AWAITS!

DATE(S) VISITED:

TRAVEL COMPANION(S):

WEATHER:

LODGINGS:

NATIONAL PARK PASSPORT STAMP

NATIONAL PARK PASSPORT STAMP

ON THE TRAIL

MY FAVORITE WALKS, HIKES, AND VIEWS

1.

2.

3.

4.

FLORA & FAUNA

THE MOST EXCITING PLANTS AND ANIMALS I SPOTTED ON MY TRIP

1.

2.

3.

4.

TAKE NOTHING BUT MEMORIES

MEMORABLE MOMENTS FROM MY TRIP

PARK RATING ☆ ☆ ☆ ☆ ☆

PLANNING A RETURN TRIP?

YES ☐ NO ☐

BADLANDS NATIONAL PARK

ESTABLISHED: 1978 (1939) • SIZE: 379 SQUARE MILES • LOCATION: SOUTHWESTERN SOUTH DAKOTA
ANCESTRAL LAND OF THE LAKOTA PEOPLE
FOR MORE INFORMATION: NPS.GOV/BADL

Other than muddy water unsuitable for drinking, there's not so much bad about Badlands National Park. The park protects the abundance of fossils within the land's geological formations while allowing specific scientific and educational institutions to excavate in the pursuit of educational, geological, and zoological observation, so scientists can study the evolution of mammal species such as the horse, rhino, and saber-toothed cat. The park also preserves the largest, protected mixed-grass prairie in the United States, located on the edge of the Great Plains, that is home to many species of wildlife, including bison and one of the most endangered mammals in North America, the black-footed ferret. The climate in the park is often unpredictable, with year-round extreme temperatures between -40°F and 116°F, though spring and fall are the best times to visit.

The Bucket List Traveler Tip READ UP ON THE HISTORY OF STRONGHOLD UNIT AND THE WOUNDED KNEE MASSACRE. A MORE MEANINGFUL WAY TO VISIT THIS PARTICULAR UNIT AT THE PARK IS BY REACHING OUT TO THE PINE RIDGE AREA CHAMBER OF COMMERCE TO JOIN A FAMILIARIZATION TOUR OR CONTACT TATANKA REZ TOURZ, THE ONLY NATIVE AMERICAN–OWNED TOUR COMPANY IN SOUTH DAKOTA.

ADVENTURE AWAITS!

DATE(S) VISITED:

TRAVEL COMPANION(S):

WEATHER:

LODGINGS:

NATIONAL PARK   PASSPORT STAMP

NATIONAL PARK   PASSPORT STAMP

ON THE TRAIL

MY FAVORITE WALKS, HIKES, AND VIEWS

1.   3.

2.   4.

FLORA & FAUNA

THE MOST EXCITING PLANTS AND ANIMALS I SPOTTED ON MY TRIP

1.   3.

2.   4.

TAKE NOTHING BUT MEMORIES

MEMORABLE MOMENTS FROM MY TRIP

PARK RATING ☆ ☆ ☆ ☆ ☆   PLANNING A
                              RETURN TRIP?   YES ☐   NO ☐

SOUTHWEST

This region, including Arkansas, New Mexico, and Texas, may be smaller in park count, but the diversity of the landscapes and the sheer size of the area are rather large. Underground, you'll find one of the deepest and longest caves in North America. Aboveground, you'll find the largest gypsum dunefield in the world. Speaking of huge, here you'll find the only national park to have an entire mountain range within its border and the largest Chihuahuan Desert protected region in the country. At one of these national parks, you can even cross a river on foot to traverse an international border into Mexico. One fact not known to many is that the oldest area in the National Park Service system is located in this region—and no, it is not Yellowstone or Yosemite.

Arkansas
- [ ] HOT SPRINGS NATIONAL PARK

New Mexico
- [ ] CARLSBAD CAVERN NATIONAL PARK
- [ ] WHITE SANDS NATIONAL PARK

Texas
- [ ] BIG BEND NATIONAL PARK
- [ ] GUADALUPE MOUNTAINS NATIONAL PARK

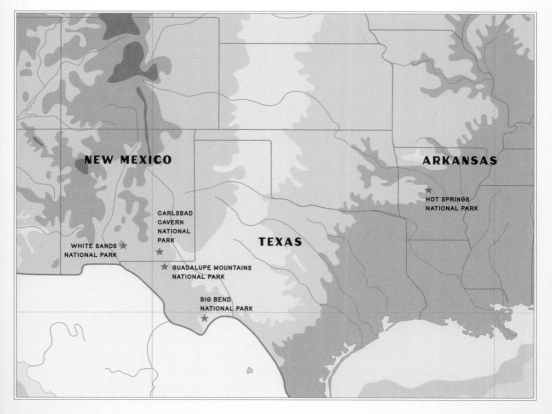

NEW MEXICO

ARKANSAS

HOT SPRINGS
NATIONAL PARK

CARLSBAD
CAVERN
NATIONAL
PARK

TEXAS

WHITE SANDS
NATIONAL PARK

GUADALUPE MOUNTAINS
NATIONAL PARK

BIG BEND
NATIONAL PARK

HOT SPRINGS NATIONAL PARK

ESTABLISHED: 1921 • SIZE: 9 SQUARE MILES • LOCATION: CENTRAL ARKANSAS
ANCESTRAL LAND OF THE QUAPAW, OSAGE, AND CADDO PEOPLES
FOR MORE INFORMATION: NPS.GOV/HOSP

Hot Springs National Park, the "American Spa," is where history and nature meet. This park is the only NPS unit mandated to give away its primary natural resource to the general public in an unending and unaltered state. Centuries before settlers arrived, Indigenous peoples enjoyed the benefits of the springs and quarried novaculite (sedimentary rock) for their tools and weapons. Once known as Hot Springs Reservation, the park was first federally set aside in 1832 to protect its primary resource, 47 natural geothermal hot springs that emerge from Hot Springs Mountain at an average temperature of 143°F. This was an early version of the national park idea, as it was the first area in the United States set aside for its natural features by the federal government. The park is located in the historic district of Hot Springs, Arkansas, where weather is fairly mild, though summer is known to be very hot and humid and prone to sudden weather.

The Bucket List Traveler Tip THIS PARK IS OFTEN RATED LOW ON THE CONVENTIONAL NATIONAL PARK LOVER'S LIST BUT I GENUINELY HAD A GREAT TIME HERE. WHERE ELSE CAN YOU FIND A TRADITIONAL BATHHOUSE PROVIDING SERVICES THAT ARE CENTURIES OLD AND USING THE AREA'S NATURAL RESOURCES AT A NATIONAL PARK? I HIGHLY RECOMMEND THE TRADITIONAL BATHING PACKAGE AT THE BUCKSTAFF BATHHOUSE.

ADVENTURE AWAITS!

DATE(S) VISITED:

TRAVEL COMPANION(S):

WEATHER:

LODGINGS:

NATIONAL PARK PASSPORT STAMP

NATIONAL PARK PASSPORT STAMP

ON THE TRAIL

MY FAVORITE WALKS, HIKES, AND VIEWS

1.   3.

2.   4.

FLORA & FAUNA

THE MOST EXCITING PLANTS AND ANIMALS I SPOTTED ON MY TRIP

1.   3.

2.   4.

TAKE NOTHING BUT MEMORIES

MEMORABLE MOMENTS FROM MY TRIP

PARK RATING ☆ ☆ ☆ ☆ ☆

PLANNING A RETURN TRIP?   YES ☐   NO ☐

CARLSBAD CAVERN NATIONAL PARK

ESTABLISHED: 1930 • SIZE: 73 SQUARE MILES • LOCATION: SOUTHEASTERN NEW MEXICO
ANCESTRAL LAND OF THE MESCALERO APACHE PEOPLE
FOR MORE INFORMATION: NPS.GOV/CACA

Who knew that under the Guadalupe Mountains and Chihuahuan Desert you'd find hidden treasures deep beneath the ground? Seven hundred and fifty feet deep, to be exact. Carlsbad Cavern contains some of the largest caves in North America. Created when sulfuric acid dissolved the surrounding limestone, it's believed the caves began forming about 4 million years ago, in tandem with the uplift of the Guadalupe Mountains. At some points during the caves' creation, a surface collapse created the Natural Entrance we see aboveground today. This park is geologically and ecologically significant for the unusual way its cave system formed (from sulfuric acid instead of carbonic acid) and the abundance of bats that call this place home during the summer. From late May through October, visitors can join the evening Bat Flight Program to witness bats taking flight in search of their dinner. Dawn of the Bats is on the third Saturday of July each year, when visitors gather at dawn to watch the bats dive back into the darkness of the cavern.

The Bucket List Traveler Tip A TWO-FER NATIONAL PARK VISIT IS CONVENIENT FOR BUCKET LIST CHECKING AND SLEEPING ARRANGEMENTS. DURING MY FIRST VISIT HERE, I SCORED A CAMPSITE AT PINE SPRINGS CAMPGROUND AT GUADALUPE MOUNTAINS NATIONAL PARK FOR TWO NIGHTS. BECAUSE THE TWO PARKS ARE ROUGHLY 40 MINUTES APART, I WAS ABLE TO HOP BETWEEN BOTH PARKS DURING MY VISIT.

ADVENTURE AWAITS!

DATE(S) VISITED:

TRAVEL COMPANION(S):

WEATHER:

LODGINGS:

NATIONAL PARK PASSPORT STAMP

NATIONAL PARK PASSPORT STAMP

ON THE TRAIL

MY FAVORITE WALKS, HIKES, AND VIEWS

1.   3.

2.   4.

FLORA & FAUNA

THE MOST EXCITING PLANTS AND ANIMALS I SPOTTED ON MY TRIP

1.   3.

2.   4.

TAKE NOTHING BUT MEMORIES

MEMORABLE MOMENTS FROM MY TRIP

PARK RATING ☆ ☆ ☆ ☆ ☆

PLANNING A
RETURN TRIP?   YES ☐ NO ☐

WHITE SANDS NATIONAL PARK

ESTABLISHED: 1933 • SIZE: 225 SQUARE MILES • LOCATION: SOUTHERN NEW MEXICO
ANCESTRAL LAND OF THE MESCALERO APACHE, TAMPACHOA (MANSOS), AND PIRO PEOPLES
FOR MORE INFORMATION: NPS.GOV/WHSA

White Sands National Park is home to the largest gypsum dunefield in the world, so large that it can be seen from space. Initially created as a national monument, the park's redesignation as a national park recognizes the added significance of its natural and cultural resources, which include Earth's largest collection of Ice Age fossilized footprints, revealing more than 20,000 years of human presence. Gypsum is rarely found as sand because it dissolves when it comes into contact with water. These sands form after the playa in the park's western end that has very high mineral content filled with water. As water evaporates, gypsum deposits are formed before getting carried away by wind, eventually forming white sand dunes. Every year since 1992, the Alamogordo Center of Commerce has hosted the most spectacular airlift in southern New Mexico on the third weekend in September, when colorful balloons rise into the air from inside the park.

The Bucket List Traveler Tip IF YOU ONLY HAVE TIME TO DRIVE THROUGH THE PARK WHILE PASSING BY THE AREA, A LOOP AROUND DUNES DRIVE PROVIDES BREATHTAKING VISTAS THAT WILL MAKE YOU FEEL LIKE YOU'RE DRIVING THROUGH ANOTHER PLANET. IT'S EXCEPTIONALLY BEAUTIFUL, ESPECIALLY IF YOU CAN TIME YOUR VISIT DURING SUNSET.

ADVENTURE AWAITS!

DATE(S) VISITED:

TRAVEL COMPANION(S):

WEATHER:

LODGINGS:

NATIONAL PARK PASSPORT STAMP

NATIONAL PARK PASSPORT STAMP

ON THE TRAIL

MY FAVORITE WALKS, HIKES, AND VIEWS

1.

2.

3.

4.

FLORA & FAUNA

THE MOST EXCITING PLANTS AND ANIMALS I SPOTTED ON MY TRIP

1.

2.

3.

4.

TAKE NOTHING BUT MEMORIES

MEMORABLE MOMENTS FROM MY TRIP

PARK RATING ☆ ☆ ☆ ☆ ☆

PLANNING A
RETURN TRIP?   YES ☐   NO ☐

BIG BEND NATIONAL PARK

ESTABLISHED: 1944 • SIZE: 1,252 SQUARE MILES • LOCATION: SOUTHWEST TEXAS
ANCESTRAL LAND OF THE CHISOS, MESCALERO APACHE, AND COMANCHE PEOPLES
FOR MORE INFORMATION: NPS.GOV/BIBE

Named for the vast curve of the Rio Grande along the Texas-Mexico border, this park is a biodiversity sanctuary. More than 1,200 species of plants, 450 species of birds, 75 species of mammals, and 56 species of reptiles reside here. Big Bend was established to preserve the largest tract of the arid Chihuahuan Desert ecology. It's the only national park in the country that contains a complete mountain range, the Chisos Mountains. Here you'll find a geological marvel evidenced in sea fossils and dinosaur bones as well as volcanic dikes that stand out in the desert landscape. There is great geographical contrast within the park, including the unique resources and vegetations along the river, the sparseness of the Chihuahuan Desert, the peaks of the Chisos Mountains, and the limestone outcrops of Boquillas Canyon.

The Bucket List Traveler Tip SHORT ON TIME? HIT THE ROSS MAXWELL SCENIC DRIVE ENDING IN SANTA ELENA CANYON. STRETCH YOUR LEGS AND HIKE THE SHORT TRAIL INTO THE CANYON. PULL OVER AT MULE EARS VIEWPOINT FOR THE ICONIC VIEW, THEN DRIVE UP TO CHISOS BASIN FOR A QUICK PEEK FROM THE WINDOW VIEW TRAIL.

ADVENTURE AWAITS!

DATE(S) VISITED:

TRAVEL COMPANION(S):

WEATHER:

LODGINGS:

NATIONAL PARK PASSPORT STAMP

NATIONAL PARK PASSPORT STAMP

ON THE TRAIL

MY FAVORITE WALKS, HIKES, AND VIEWS

1.   3.

2.   4.

FLORA & FAUNA

THE MOST EXCITING PLANTS AND ANIMALS I SPOTTED ON MY TRIP

1.   3.

2.   4.

TAKE NOTHING BUT MEMORIES

MEMORABLE MOMENTS FROM MY TRIP

PARK RATING ☆ ☆ ☆ ☆ ☆   PLANNING A RETURN TRIP?   YES ☐ NO ☐

GUADALUPE MOUNTAINS NATIONAL PARK

ESTABLISHED: 1972 • SIZE: 135 SQUARE MILES • LOCATION: WEST TEXAS
ANCESTRAL LAND OF THE MESCALERO APACHE PEOPLE
FOR MORE INFORMATION: NPS.GOV/GUMO

Home to the highest natural point in Texas and the world's most extensive Permian fossil reef, Guadalupe Mountains National Park preserves a landscape that holds outstanding geological value. From reef to peaks, the park's rugged beauty is comprised of a desert mountain environment, including McKittrick Canyon, a riparian waterway that prompts premier leaf foliage in the fall, its namesake mountains that rise more than 3,000 feet above the arid Chihuahuan Desert, and Salt Basin Dunes that are remnants of an ancient lake from nearly 2 million years ago. As part of settler history, the park also houses ruins of an old stagecoach station and the restored Frijole Ranch, which hosts a museum of ranching history. This park has witnessed 10,000 years of human history.

The Bucket List Traveler Tip PLANNING TO HIKE UP TO GUADALUPE PEAK OR EL CAPITAN? GET AN EARLY START AND BEAT THE CROWD (AND SUN) BY CAMPING NEXT TO THE TRAILHEAD AT PINE SPRINGS CAMPGROUND. IT'S A LONG HIKE, SO BRING ENOUGH WATER AND SNACKS.

ADVENTURE AWAITS!

DATE(S) VISITED:

TRAVEL COMPANION(S):

WEATHER:

LODGINGS:

NATIONAL PARK PASSPORT STAMP

NATIONAL PARK PASSPORT STAMP

ON THE TRAIL

MY FAVORITE WALKS, HIKES, AND VIEWS

1.

2.

3.

4.

FLORA & FAUNA

THE MOST EXCITING PLANTS AND ANIMALS I SPOTTED ON MY TRIP

1.

2.

3.

4.

TAKE NOTHING BUT MEMORIES

MEMORABLE MOMENTS FROM MY TRIP

PARK RATING ☆ ☆ ☆ ☆ ☆

PLANNING A RETURN TRIP?

YES ☐ NO ☐

MIDWEST

This region sees no shortage in bodies of water, which are the foundation of all five national parks across Indiana, Michigan, Minnesota, Missouri, and Ohio. Between the lakes and the rivers that served as critical transportation hubs back in the 1800s, the parks here pack in a lot of human and Earth history dating back to time immemorial, from the period when Indigenous peoples thrived to the arrival of explorers, settlers, and slaves, which historically changed the trajectory of the country.

Indiana
☐ INDIANA DUNES NATIONAL PARK

Michigan
☐ ISLE ROYALE NATIONAL PARK

Minnesota
☐ VOYAGEURS NATIONAL PARK

Missouri
☐ GATEWAY ARCH NATIONAL PARK

Ohio
☐ CUYAHOGA VALLEY NATIONAL PARK

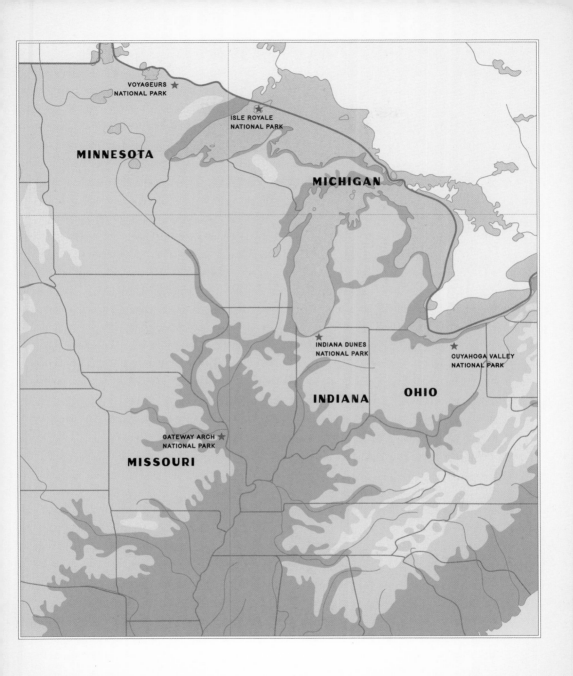

VOYAGEURS
NATIONAL PARK

MINNESOTA

ISLE ROYALE
NATIONAL PARK

MICHIGAN

INDIANA DUNES
NATIONAL PARK

CUYAHOGA VALLEY
NATIONAL PARK

INDIANA

OHIO

GATEWAY ARCH
NATIONAL PARK

MISSOURI

INDIANA DUNES NATIONAL PARK

ESTABLISHED: 1966 • SIZE: 24 SQUARE MILES • LOCATION: NORTHWESTERN INDIANA
ANCESTRAL LAND OF THE MIAMI, PEORIA, MAHICAN, MASCOUTEN, MESKWAKI, SAUK, SHAWNEE,
KIIKAAPOI, KASKASKIA, IROQUOIS, AND POTAWATOMI PEOPLES
FOR MORE INFORMATION: NPS.GOV/INDU

Indiana Dunes National Park protects one of the most biologically diverse habitats in the nation. Home to more than 1,000 species of plants, more than 350 species of birds, and the federally endangered Karner blue butterfly, it is located within several ecological transition zones, and the moderating effect of Lake Michigan explains much of the plant and animal diversity. This was the birthplace of ecology, the study of the relationships between living organisms and their physical environment. The park landscape represents at least four major successive stages of historic Lake Michigan shorelines, making it one of the most extensive geologic records of one of the world's largest freshwater bodies. The park hosts its annual birding festival in May to celebrate the migration of birdlife through the region.

The Bucket List Traveler Tip EVERY FRIDAY IN THE LATE AFTERNOON, YOU CAN JOIN A RANGER-LED HIKE TO THE TOP OF MOUNT BALDY, A MASSIVE SAND DUNE TOWERING 126 FEET ABOVE LAKE MICHIGAN. THIS AREA IS ONLY ACCESSIBLE TO THE PUBLIC DURING THESE HIKES DUE TO PUBLIC SAFETY AND RESTORATION EFFORTS.

ADVENTURE AWAITS!

DATE(S) VISITED:

TRAVEL COMPANION(S):

WEATHER:

LODGINGS:

NATIONAL PARK PASSPORT STAMP

NATIONAL PARK PASSPORT STAMP

ON THE TRAIL

MY FAVORITE WALKS, HIKES, AND VIEWS

1.

2.

3.

4.

FLORA & FAUNA

THE MOST EXCITING PLANTS AND ANIMALS I SPOTTED ON MY TRIP

1.

2.

3.

4.

TAKE NOTHING BUT MEMORIES

MEMORABLE MOMENTS FROM MY TRIP

PARK RATING ☆ ☆ ☆ ☆ ☆

PLANNING A RETURN TRIP?

YES ☐ NO ☐

ISLE ROYALE NATIONAL PARK

ESTABLISHED: 1940 • SIZE: 893 SQUARE MILES • LOCATION: NORTHERN MICHIGAN
ANCESTRAL LAND OF THE OJIBWE, CREE, AND ASSINIBOINE PEOPLES
FOR MORE INFORMATION: NPS.GOV/ISRO

If you're seeking solitude, you'll find it in the superior wilderness, cool climate, and crystal-clear waters of Isle Royale National Park. Nestled at the northern end of Lake Superior, the park is only accessible by boat or seaplane. This rugged, 45-mile-long and 9-mile-wide isolated island is home to more than 1,300 moose and approximately 30 gray wolves. Here, the sound of wolves howling is a unique aspect of the remote island experience. With more than 80 percent of the park underwater, Isle Royale preserves a remote island archipelago and the surrounding waters of Lake Superior. The park is closed to all visitors from November to mid-April. Starting in early July and running through early September, there are a half dozen tours and programs available (for a fee) aboard the *MV Sandy* sightseeing boat from Rock Harbor.

The Bucket List Traveler Tip BETWEEN THE COMPLEX LOGISTICS AND THE COST TO GET THERE, THE PARK ISN'T VERY POPULAR. I RECOMMEND AT A MINIMUM AN OVERNIGHT TRIP TO APPRECIATE ITS ESSENCE (ROCK HARBOR IS A SOLID CHOICE), THOUGH A DAY TRIP IS DOABLE FROM GRAND PORTAGE AT A REASONABLE COST ABOARD *SEA HUNTER III*. BE PREPARED FOR A ROUGH BOAT RIDE.

ADVENTURE AWAITS!

DATE(S) VISITED:

TRAVEL COMPANION(S):

WEATHER:

LODGINGS:

NATIONAL PARK PASSPORT STAMP

NATIONAL PARK PASSPORT STAMP

ON THE TRAIL

MY FAVORITE WALKS, HIKES, AND VIEWS

1.   3.

2.   4.

FLORA & FAUNA

THE MOST EXCITING PLANTS AND ANIMALS I SPOTTED ON MY TRIP

1.   3.

2.   4.

TAKE NOTHING BUT MEMORIES

MEMORABLE MOMENTS FROM MY TRIP

PARK RATING ☆ ☆ ☆ ☆ ☆   **PLANNING A RETURN TRIP?**   YES ☐   NO ☐

VOYAGEURS NATIONAL PARK

ESTABLISHED: 1975 • SIZE: 341 SQUARE MILES • LOCATION: NORTHERN MINNESOTA
ANCESTRAL LAND OF THE CREE, MONSONI, ASSINIBOINE, AND OJIBWE PEOPLES
FOR MORE INFORMATION: NPS.GOV/VOYA

Voyageur means "traveler" in French, and Voyageurs National Park calls to travelers seeking adventures beyond the shoreline. Water makes up more than one-third of the park, making it primarily accessible by boat and via snowmobiles in wintertime. Within its boundaries, more than 30 lakes fill up the glacier-carved rock basins that were once routes for travel and the fur trade. The four large, interconnected lakes—Rainy, Kabetogama, Namakan, and Sand Point—along with other smaller lakes cover almost 40 percent of the park's area. The park protects a unique cultural history that was shaped by the rugged nature of its water and lands, and you can see and touch rock outcrops that are half the age of Earth. The ranger-led North Canoe Voyage is the most unique educational experience here, immersing visitors in a living history lesson by costumed and spirited interpretive rangers paddling back in history.

The Bucket List Traveler Tip IF YOU WANT TO EXPERIENCE THE PARK WITHOUT ALL THE PADDLING, JOIN THE NATURALIST-GUIDED TOUR WITH PARK RANGERS. KETTLE FALLS CRUISE (FROM RAINY LAKE OR ASH RIVER VISITOR CENTERS) IS THE BEST SELECTION, GIVING YOU THE MOST EXPLORATION TIME BY LAND AND WATER WHILE LEARNING ABOUT THE CULTURAL AND NATURAL HISTORY OF THE PARK.

ADVENTURE AWAITS!

DATE(S) VISITED:

TRAVEL COMPANION(S):

WEATHER:

LODGINGS:

NATIONAL PARK PASSPORT STAMP

NATIONAL PARK PASSPORT STAMP

ON THE TRAIL

MY FAVORITE WALKS, HIKES, AND VIEWS

1.

2.

3.

4.

FLORA & FAUNA

THE MOST EXCITING PLANTS AND ANIMALS I SPOTTED ON MY TRIP

1.

2.

3.

4.

TAKE NOTHING BUT MEMORIES

MEMORABLE MOMENTS FROM MY TRIP

PARK RATING ☆ ☆ ☆ ☆ ☆

PLANNING A
RETURN TRIP?   YES ☐   NO ☐

GATEWAY ARCH NATIONAL PARK

ESTABLISHED: 1935 • SIZE: 0.14 SQUARE MILES • LOCATION: EASTERN MISSOURI
ANCESTRAL LAND OF THE KIIKAAPOI, KASKASKIA, OSAGE, MYAAMIA, AND O-GA-XPA PEOPLES
FOR MORE INFORMATION: NPS.GOV/JEFF

Standing 630 feet tall, this arch has the distinction of being the world's tallest arch. Endearingly known as the "Gateway to the West," the park was established when President Franklin D. Roosevelt designated property along the St. Louis riverfront to be developed as Jefferson National Expansion Memorial. Stretching from the Old Courthouse to the steps overlooking the Mississippi River, Gateway Arch National Park offers a different perspective for a national park. Rather than expansive views of the mountains or miles of hiking trails, this urban park unpacks centuries of history that shaped the region and the country. The Museum at the Gateway Arch covers more than 200 years of history about the United States' westward expansion, told from diverse perspectives, with an emphasis on St. Louis's critical role in that era. On the last Saturday in May, park staff and volunteers dressed in eighteenth-century clothing share the story of the British/Indian attack on St. Louis that took place at the present-day Gateway Arch on May 26, 1780.

The Bucket List Traveler Tip STAY AT THE HYATT REGENCY ST. LOUIS AT THE ARCH. NOT ONLY IS THE LOCATION CONVENIENT (ESPECIALLY FOR A MIDDAY NAP WHILE YOU WAIT OUT THE CROWD), BUT THE VIEWS FROM THE ROOMS CAN BE ABSOLUTELY AMAZING. SPEND THE EXTRA FUNDS TO UPGRADE YOUR ROOM TO THE "ARCH VIEW" ROOM.

ADVENTURE AWAITS!

DATE(S) VISITED:

TRAVEL COMPANION(S):

WEATHER:

LODGINGS:

NATIONAL PARK PASSPORT STAMP

NATIONAL PARK PASSPORT STAMP

ON THE TRAIL

MY FAVORITE WALKS, HIKES, AND VIEWS

1.   3.

2.   4.

FLORA & FAUNA

THE MOST EXCITING PLANTS AND ANIMALS I SPOTTED ON MY TRIP

1.   3.

2.   4.

TAKE NOTHING BUT MEMORIES

MEMORABLE MOMENTS FROM MY TRIP

PARK RATING ☆ ☆ ☆ ☆ ☆

PLANNING A
RETURN TRIP?   YES ☐   NO ☐

CUYAHOGA VALLEY NATIONAL PARK

ESTABLISHED: 1974 • SIZE: 51 SQUARE MILES • LOCATION: NORTHEAST OHIO
ANCESTRAL LAND OF THE IROQUOIS, MOHAWK, MUNSEE, SHAWNEE, AND LENAPE PEOPLES
FOR MORE INFORMATION: NPS.GOV/CUVA

Sparked by the Cuyahoga River catching on fire in the late 1960s due to water pollution, Congress established Cuyahoga Valley National Park as part of Parks to the People, a civil rights initiative to create national parks in metropolitan areas. The park protects 22 miles of the river between Akron and Cleveland and the surrounding area along the river from being consumed by development expansion, as well as preserving the history of the Ohio and Erie Canals. In the early 1800s, water from the lower Cuyahoga River was diverted for the Erie Canal, which was, for a few decades, an important link for the inland shipping network. The Ohio Canal was constructed soon after. Remains of both canals offer glimpses into the history of how this part of the country was transformed.

The Bucket List Traveler Tip IF YOU ONLY HAVE A DAY TO VISIT, HERE ARE THE THREE MUST-DOS: THE LEDGES, BLUE HEN FALLS, AND BRANDYWINE FALLS. IF YOU CAN PICK THE TIME OF YEAR, FALL IS THE MOST MAGICAL. STOP BY ON FRIDAY OR MONDAY AND SKIP THE WEEKEND CROWD.

ADVENTURE AWAITS!

DATE(S) VISITED:
....

TRAVEL COMPANION(S):
....
....

NATIONAL PARK PASSPORT STAMP

NATIONAL PARK PASSPORT STAMP

WEATHER:
....

LODGINGS:
....

ON THE TRAIL

MY FAVORITE WALKS, HIKES, AND VIEWS

1.   3.

2.   4.

FLORA & FAUNA

THE MOST EXCITING PLANTS AND ANIMALS I SPOTTED ON MY TRIP

1.   3.

2.   4.

TAKE NOTHING BUT MEMORIES

MEMORABLE MOMENTS FROM MY TRIP

....
....
....
....
....
....
....
....
....
....

PARK RATING ☆ ☆ ☆ ☆ ☆   **PLANNING A RETURN TRIP?**   **YES** ☐ **NO** ☐

SOUTHEAST

From caves to swamp land to pristine beaches, the Southeast region has quite the variation of landscape to offer, depending on what you're packing for your vacation. Underground, the world's longest known cave system is found here. Underwater, you'll find the third-largest coral barrier reef in the world and the only tropical reef in the continental United States. Surrounded by pristine blue water is one of the largest forts ever built. Do not disregard the beauty of wetlands, either, as they're home to the largest mangrove ecosystem in the Western Hemisphere, the largest continuous strand of sawgrass prairie, and the most significant breeding ground for wading birds in North America. Included in this section are the national parks located in Florida, Kentucky, North and South Carolina, Tennessee, and the US Virgin Islands.

Florida

- ☐ BISCAYNE NATIONAL PARK
- ☐ DRY TORTUGAS NATIONAL PARK
- ☐ EVERGLADES NATIONAL PARK

Kentucky

- ☐ MAMMOTH CAVE NATIONAL PARK

North Carolina/Tennessee

- ☐ GREAT SMOKY MOUNTAINS NATIONAL PARK

South Carolina

- ☐ CONGAREE NATIONAL PARK

Virgin Islands

- ☐ VIRGIN ISLANDS NATIONAL PARK

VIRGIN ISLANDS

VIRGIN ISLANDS
NATIONAL PARK ★

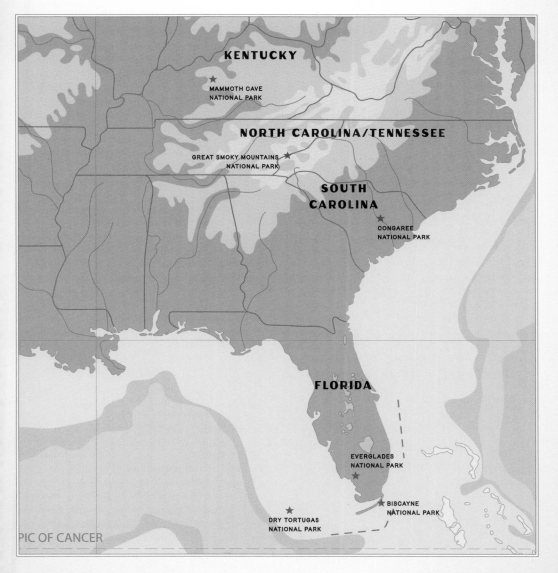

KENTUCKY

★
MAMMOTH CAVE
NATIONAL PARK

NORTH CAROLINA/TENNESSEE

GREAT SMOKY MOUNTAINS ★
NATIONAL PARK

**SOUTH
CAROLINA**

★
CONGAREE
NATIONAL PARK

FLORIDA

EVERGLADES
NATIONAL PARK
★

★
DRY TORTUGAS
NATIONAL PARK

★ BISCAYNE
NATIONAL PARK

PIC OF CANCER

BISCAYNE NATIONAL PARK

ESTABLISHED: 1980 (1968) • SIZE: 270 SQUARE MILES • LOCATION: FLORIDA KEYS
ANCESTRAL LAND OF THE TEQUESTA, TAINO, AND SEMINOLE PEOPLES
FOR MORE INFORMATION: NPS.GOV/BISC

Biscayne National Park is a warm, watery wonderland, protecting a rare combination of terrestrial, tropical, marine, and amphibious life. With 95 percent of the park underwater, Biscayne is home to an incredible diversity of life from more than 600 native fish species to neotropical water birds and many threatened and endangered species, including the West Indian manatee, American crocodile, and five species of sea turtles. As for flora, you'll see Florida semaphore cactus and buccaneer palm, considered the rarest palm native to Florida. The reefs of Biscayne National Park are the only living coral reefs in the continental United States, part of a 150-mile-long chain of coral reefs extending down through the lower Florida Keys and the Caribbean. The entrance to the park is located in Homestead, Florida, where you can stop by for park orientation at the visitor center before heading out into the water by boat, kayak, or a guided boat tour by the Biscayne National Park Institute (fee required).

The Bucket List Traveler Tip TO GET A TASTE OF THE PARK (LITERALLY, AS YOU MAY ACCIDENTALLY GULP THE SEAWATER), I RECOMMEND THE JONES LAGOON ECO-ADVENTURE WITH BISCAYNE NATIONAL PARK INSTITUTE. YOU'LL BE PADDLEBOARDING IN CALM AND CLEAR WATER AT . . . YOU GUESSED IT, JONES LAGOON. IT WAS A MEMORABLE EXPERIENCE FOR THIS FIRST-TIME PADDLEBOARDER.

ADVENTURE AWAITS!

DATE(S) VISITED:

TRAVEL COMPANION(S):

WEATHER:

LODGINGS:

NATIONAL PARK PASSPORT STAMP

NATIONAL PARK PASSPORT STAMP

ON THE TRAIL

MY FAVORITE WALKS, HIKES, AND VIEWS

1.   3.

2.   4.

FLORA & FAUNA

THE MOST EXCITING PLANTS AND ANIMALS I SPOTTED ON MY TRIP

1.   3.

2.   4.

TAKE NOTHING BUT MEMORIES

MEMORABLE MOMENTS FROM MY TRIP

PARK RATING ☆ ☆ ☆ ☆ ☆   PLANNING A RETURN TRIP?   YES ☐ NO ☐

DRY TORTUGAS NATIONAL PARK

ESTABLISHED: 1992 (1935) • SIZE: 100 SQUARE MILES • LOCATION: FLORIDA KEYS
ANCESTRAL LAND OF THE SEMINOLE PEOPLE
FOR MORE INFORMATION: NPS.GOV/DRTO

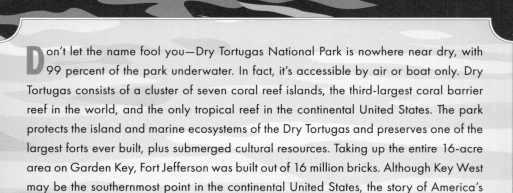

Don't let the name fool you—Dry Tortugas National Park is nowhere near dry, with 99 percent of the park underwater. In fact, it's accessible by air or boat only. Dry Tortugas consists of a cluster of seven coral reef islands, the third-largest coral barrier reef in the world, and the only tropical reef in the continental United States. The park protects the island and marine ecosystems of the Dry Tortugas and preserves one of the largest forts ever built, plus submerged cultural resources. Taking up the entire 16-acre area on Garden Key, Fort Jefferson was built out of 16 million bricks. Although Key West may be the southernmost point in the continental United States, the story of America's cultural heritage and maritime history go beyond the zero mile marker of US-1.

The Bucket List Traveler Tip DON'T LET THIS PARK BE A "SOMEDAY" THAT BECOMES A "NEVER." IF YOU'RE ALREADY IN THE MIAMI AREA TO VISIT EVERGLADES AND BISCAYNE, SQUEEZE THIS ONE IN. I COMBINED MY VISIT WITH BISCAYNE AND EVERGLADES, ALONG WITH BIG CYPRESS NATIONAL PRESERVE, OVER A THREE-DAY WEEKEND.

ADVENTURE AWAITS!

DATE(S) VISITED:

TRAVEL COMPANION(S):

WEATHER:

LODGINGS:

NATIONAL PARK PASSPORT STAMP

NATIONAL PARK PASSPORT STAMP

ON THE TRAIL

MY FAVORITE WALKS, HIKES, AND VIEWS

1.   3.

2.   4.

FLORA & FAUNA

THE MOST EXCITING PLANTS AND ANIMALS I SPOTTED ON MY TRIP

1.   3.

2.   4.

TAKE NOTHING BUT MEMORIES

MEMORABLE MOMENTS FROM MY TRIP

PARK RATING ☆ ☆ ☆ ☆ ☆   PLANNING A RETURN TRIP?   YES ☐ NO ☐

EVERGLADES NATIONAL PARK

ESTABLISHED: 1947 • SIZE: 2,410 SQUARE MILES • LOCATION: SOUTHERN FLORIDA
ANCESTRAL LAND OF THE SEMINOLE, MICCOSUKEE, CALUSA, TEQUESTA, TAINO, JEGA, AND AIS PEOPLES
FOR MORE INFORMATION: NPS.GOV/EVER

Known as Pa-hay-Okee (grassy waters) by the Indigenous peoples in the area, Everglades National Park is home to one of the world's largest wetlands. The park protects a unique ecosystem of mangrove forests, tropical hardwood hammocks, and freshwater prairies, along with hundreds of bird, animal, and plant species. Its junctures at the interface of temperate climate and subtropical America, fresh and brackish water, shallow bays and deeper coastal waters, contribute to a conglomerate of habitats supporting significant diversity of flora and fauna. Prior to its protection, the Everglades territory was drained in the 1800s for development. Today, this vast habitat has been declared a World Heritage Site and an International Biosphere Reserve. The park has two seasons: dry (November to March) and wet (April to October). And remember, hurricane season begins in June and lasts until November.

The Bucket List Traveler Tip THE ANHINGA TRAIL IS GORGEOUS, BUT THE VULTURES ACTING AS THE WELCOMING COMMITTEE AT THE PARKING LOT—NOT THAT GREAT. (NO PUN INTENDED, THOUGH A GROUP OF VULTURES *IS* CALLED A "COMMITTEE.") PROTECT YOUR VEHICLE FROM POTENTIAL DAMAGE USING TARPS AND BUNGEE CORDS. COVER EXPOSED RUBBER WITH A WET SHEET OR TOWEL AND PARK IN FULL SUN.

ADVENTURE AWAITS!

DATE(S) VISITED:

TRAVEL COMPANION(S):

WEATHER:

LODGINGS:

NATIONAL PARK PASSPORT STAMP

NATIONAL PARK PASSPORT STAMP

ON THE TRAIL

MY FAVORITE WALKS, HIKES, AND VIEWS

1.

2.

3.

4.

FLORA & FAUNA

THE MOST EXCITING PLANTS AND ANIMALS I SPOTTED ON MY TRIP

1.

2.

3.

4.

TAKE NOTHING BUT MEMORIES

MEMORABLE MOMENTS FROM MY TRIP

PARK RATING ☆ ☆ ☆ ☆ ☆

PLANNING A RETURN TRIP? YES ☐ NO ☐

MAMMOTH CAVE NATIONAL PARK

ESTABLISHED: 1941 • SIZE: 83 SQUARE MILES • LOCATION: CENTRAL KENTUCKY
ANCESTRAL LAND OF THE CHEROKEE, SHAWNEE, AND CHICKASAW PEOPLES
FOR MORE INFORMATION: NPS.GOV/MACA

Magnificent, mysterious, and absolutely mighty, Mammoth Cave National Park is home to the longest recorded cave system in the world, with more than 400 miles mapped and new caves continually being discovered. The park protects the underground labyrinth cave system, the rolling hills aboveground, the lushly deciduous forests ecosystem, and the scenic river valleys of the Green and Nolin Rivers. Inside the aptly named Mammoth Cave, you'll find tube-like as well as towering passageways, large rooms with sparkling walls, maze-like sprawl, slot canyons and large canyons, huge domes, and even a dripstone that resembles a frozen waterfall. Aboveground, thousands of plants and tree species have created a sprawling landscape that earned this park its designations as a UNESCO World Heritage Site and an International Biosphere Reserve. Cave tours and most visitor services are found on the south side of the Green River, while the north side of the park offers backcountry camping, hiking, and other aboveground outdoor activities.

The Bucket List Traveler Tip THE DOMES AND DRIPSTONE CAVE TOUR IS A CLASSIC OPTION, AND THE SELF-GUIDED DISCOVERY TOUR IS IDEAL IF YOU'RE SHORT ON TIME. RESERVE YOUR CAVE TOUR TICKET ONLINE AS THEY'RE LIMITED AND VARY THROUGH THE SEASON. WAITING TO BUY UNTIL YOU GET TO THE VISITOR CENTER RISKS A SOLD-OUT TOUR.

ADVENTURE AWAITS!

DATE(S) VISITED:

TRAVEL COMPANION(S):

WEATHER:

LODGINGS:

NATIONAL PARK PASSPORT STAMP

NATIONAL PARK PASSPORT STAMP

ON THE TRAIL

MY FAVORITE WALKS, HIKES, AND VIEWS

1.   3.

2.   4.

FLORA & FAUNA

THE MOST EXCITING PLANTS AND ANIMALS I SPOTTED ON MY TRIP

1.   3.

2.   4.

TAKE NOTHING BUT MEMORIES

MEMORABLE MOMENTS FROM MY TRIP

PARK RATING ☆ ☆ ☆ ☆ ☆   **PLANNING A RETURN TRIP?**   YES ☐ NO ☐

GREAT SMOKY MOUNTAINS NATIONAL PARK

ESTABLISHED: 1934 • SIZE: 816 SQUARE MILES • LOCATION: NORTH CAROLINA–TENNESSEE BORDER
ANCESTRAL LAND OF THE CHEROKEE PEOPLE
FOR MORE INFORMATION: NPS.GOV/GRSM

Named for low-hanging fog produced in the early morning hours, Great Smoky Mountains National Park is a place where we reclaim health while conserving the environment. Around the late 1890s, the ancient Smokies had gained a reputation as a clean and cool mountain air refuge for those with respiratory ailments like tuberculosis. Today, the park protects the forest and wildlife that call it home while providing recreational space for mankind to coexist. The Great Smoky Mountains are among the oldest mountains in the world, formed approximately 200 to 300 million years ago. This mountain range is world renowned for the diversity of its plant and animal life, as well as its history of southern Appalachian mountain culture. The park's Smokiest Harvest Celebration in October highlights traditional fall pursuits that were an important part of rural life in these southern mountains.

The Bucket List Traveler Tip THE BEAUTY ABOUT BEING HERE IN THE FALL IS THAT IF YOU EXIT OR ENTER THE PARK VIA THE SOUTH ENTRANCE COMING OFF BLUE RIDGE PARKWAY, YOU'LL BE IN FALL FOLIAGE HEAVEN! EVEN IF YOU CAN'T DRIVE TOO FAR ALONG THE PARKWAY, A FEW MILES ARE ALL YOU'LL NEED TO SOAK IT IN.

ADVENTURE AWAITS!

DATE(S) VISITED:

TRAVEL COMPANION(S):

WEATHER:

LODGINGS:

NATIONAL PARK PASSPORT STAMP

NATIONAL PARK PASSPORT STAMP

ON THE TRAIL

MY FAVORITE WALKS, HIKES, AND VIEWS

1.

2.

3.

4.

FLORA & FAUNA

THE MOST EXCITING PLANTS AND ANIMALS I SPOTTED ON MY TRIP

1.

2.

3.

4.

TAKE NOTHING BUT MEMORIES

MEMORABLE MOMENTS FROM MY TRIP

PARK RATING ☆ ☆ ☆ ☆ ☆

PLANNING A RETURN TRIP?

YES ☐ NO ☐

CONGAREE NATIONAL PARK

ESTABLISHED: 2003 (1976) • SIZE: 41 SQUARE MILES • LOCATION: CENTRAL SOUTH CAROLINA
ANCESTRAL LAND OF THE CONGAREE PEOPLE
FOR MORE INFORMATION: NPS.GOV/CONG

Step into the "Redwoods of the East"! Home to some of the tallest trees on the East Coast, Congaree National Park preserves the largest remaining tract of southern old-growth bottomland hardwood forest in the United States. Water from the Congaree and Wateree Rivers sweep through this ancient alluvial floodplain, carrying nutrients and sediments that nourish and rejuvenate the ecosystem to support the growth of these deep and dense, swampy forests. The park also protects a landscape shaped by the many people who have lived on and used the floodplain for thousands of years, be it Indigenous peoples to Revolutionary War patriots to enslaved peoples seeking refuge. Seeing the synchronous fireflies at the park is the ultimate bucket list item. The park even hosts annual firefly viewing in May and June, so visitors can experience the awe-inspiring display of synchronous flashing while the insects search for their mates.

The Bucket List Traveler Tip IF VISITING IN THE SUMMER, DON'T FORGET TO BRING YOUR BUG SPRAY. BEFORE HITTING THE TRAIL, CHECK OUT THE "MOSQUITO METER" AT THE VISITOR CENTER. STARTING FROM 1 BEING ALL CLEAR TO 6 BEING THE WAR ZONE, IT'LL HELP YOU EVALUATE YOUR HIKING PLAN.

ADVENTURE AWAITS!

DATE(S) VISITED:

TRAVEL COMPANION(S):

WEATHER:

LODGINGS:

NATIONAL PARK PASSPORT STAMP

NATIONAL PARK PASSPORT STAMP

ON THE TRAIL

MY FAVORITE WALKS, HIKES, AND VIEWS

1.   3.

2.   4.

FLORA & FAUNA

THE MOST EXCITING PLANTS AND ANIMALS I SPOTTED ON MY TRIP

1.   3.

2.   4.

TAKE NOTHING BUT MEMORIES

MEMORABLE MOMENTS FROM MY TRIP

PARK RATING ☆ ☆ ☆ ☆ ☆

PLANNING A RETURN TRIP?   YES ☐   NO ☐

VIRGIN ISLANDS NATIONAL PARK

ESTABLISHED: 1956 • SIZE: 23 SQUARE MILES • LOCATION: THE CARIBBEAN
ANCESTRAL LAND OF THE TAINO (ARAWAKS), KALINAGO (CARIB), CIBONEY, AND IGNERI PEOPLES
FOR MORE INFORMATION: NPS.GOV/VIIS

Virgin Islands National Park is located on St. John, along the outskirts of the Caribbean Ocean in the US Virgin Islands. The park is home to coral reefs that are safe havens for 500 different species of fish, along with seagrass meadows and mangrove prop roots. Besides protecting the submerged lands and marine life, the park also protects some of the last remaining native tropical dry rainforest in the Caribbean and the relics of early Carib Indian culture. The complex history of civilizations here includes the enslavement of Africans on sugar plantations and the subsistence era that followed emancipation. Ruins of more than 100 plantations dating from the peak of sugar production are located within park boundaries, such as Reef Bay Sugar Factory and Annenberg Plantation. The park hosts an annual folklife festival at Annenberg Sugar Plantation Ruins during Black History Month in February, focusing on West Indian cultural traditions.

The Bucket List Traveler Tip IF YOU'RE VISITING THE US VIRGIN ISLANDS SOLELY TO SPEND TIME AT THE NATIONAL PARK, YOU WON'T NEED A CAR TO GET AROUND. THE PARK ITSELF DOESN'T PROVIDE SHUTTLES, BUT THERE ARE SHARED OPEN-AIR "SAFARI-STYLE" TAXIS (PICKUP TRUCKS WITH THE BEDS CONVERTED TO ROWS OF BENCH SEATING WITH OVERHEAD SHADE). CARRY CASH FOR THE FARE.

ADVENTURE AWAITS!

DATE(S) VISITED:

TRAVEL COMPANION(S):

WEATHER:

LODGINGS:

NATIONAL PARK PASSPORT STAMP

NATIONAL PARK PASSPORT STAMP

ON THE TRAIL

MY FAVORITE WALKS, HIKES, AND VIEWS

1.

2.

3.

4.

FLORA & FAUNA

THE MOST EXCITING PLANTS AND ANIMALS I SPOTTED ON MY TRIP

1.

2.

3.

4.

TAKE NOTHING BUT MEMORIES

MEMORABLE MOMENTS FROM MY TRIP

PARK RATING ☆ ☆ ☆ ☆ ☆

PLANNING A RETURN TRIP?

YES ☐ NO ☐

MID-ATLANTIC

The mountain ranges on this side of the US map aren't as tall as the ones to the west, but over here you'll find the oldest building blocks of our nation, which also boast the prettiest colors from spring to summer to fall. In this region, you'll learn the long history of European settlements and the area that was once the epicenter of the coal mining industry. In between the gorgeous gorges and long lines of ridges, you'll find plenty of recreational opportunities within the parks and the surrounding areas. Included in this section are the national parks located in Virginia and West Virginia.

Virginia

☐ SHENANDOAH NATIONAL PARK

West Virginia

☐ NEW RIVER GORGE NATIONAL PARK

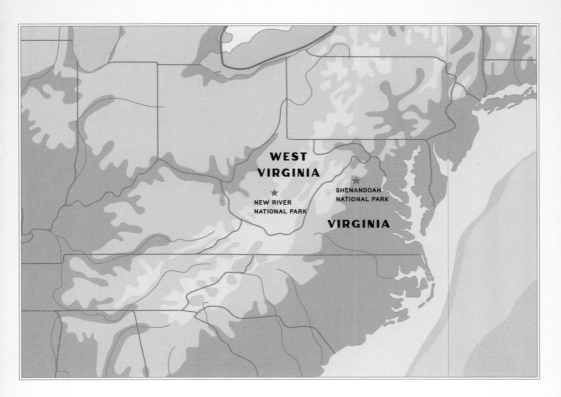

WEST
VIRGINIA

★
NEW RIVER
NATIONAL PARK

★
SHENANDOAH
NATIONAL PARK

VIRGINIA

SHENANDOAH NATIONAL PARK

ESTABLISHED: 1935 • SIZE: 311 SQUARE MILES • LOCATION: NORTHERN VIRGINIA
ANCESTRAL LAND OF THE IROQUOIS, SHAWNEE, CATAWBA, CHEROKEE, DELAWARE, SUSQUEHANNOCK,
MANAHOAC, MONACAN, AND MASSAWOMECK PEOPLES
FOR MORE INFORMATION: NPS.GOV/SHEN

They say Virginia is for lovers. This is especially true for national park lovers. Shenandoah, with its cascading waterfalls, beautiful mountain vistas, and serene woods, serves as a great escape from nearby DC's hustle and bustle. Unlike some national parks, Shenandoah is a place where settlers lived for more than a century. To create the park, Virginia state officials acquired 1,088 privately owned tracts and donated the land to the nation with the intent to preserve an area of natural beauty in the region and provide access to recreational opportunities for surrounding communities. Much of Shenandoah consisted of farmland and second- or third-growth forests logged since the early 1700s. Today, the park is considered a "recycled" park, where the land has been reclaimed from its overused original condition. The mountain is usually 10°F cooler than the valley below, so wear layers and always check the forecast so you're well prepared.

The Bucket List Traveler Tip TO MAKE THE MOST OF YOUR TIME IN THIS "SHOESTRING" PARK, STAY IN THE PARK. IF NOT CAMPING, THE CABIN OPTION IS VERY AFFORDABLE COMPARED TO IN-PARK LODGING AT NATIONAL PARKS FARTHER WEST. WITH 500 MILES OF TRAILS TO HIKE, WHY SPEND TIME COMMUTING TO AND FROM THE PARK WHILE WAITING IN LINE AT AN ENTRANCE STATION?

ADVENTURE AWAITS!

DATE(S) VISITED:

TRAVEL COMPANION(S):

NATIONAL PARK PASSPORT STAMP

NATIONAL PARK PASSPORT STAMP

WEATHER:

LODGINGS:

ON THE TRAIL

MY FAVORITE WALKS, HIKES, AND VIEWS

1.   3.

2.   4.

FLORA & FAUNA

THE MOST EXCITING PLANTS AND ANIMALS I SPOTTED ON MY TRIP

1.   3.

2.   4.

TAKE NOTHING BUT MEMORIES

MEMORABLE MOMENTS FROM MY TRIP

PARK RATING ☆ ☆ ☆ ☆ ☆   PLANNING A RETURN TRIP?   YES ☐ NO ☐

NEW RIVER GORGE NATIONAL PARK

ESTABLISHED: 1978 • SIZE: 114 SQUARE MILES • LOCATION: SOUTHERN WEST VIRGINIA
ANCESTRAL LAND OF THE EASTERN BAND OF CHEROKEE, TUTELO, YUCHI, AND MONETON PEOPLES
FOR MORE INFORMATION: NPS.GOV/NERI

Believed to be one of the oldest rivers on Earth, possibly as old as 65 million years old, New River is definitely not the newest kid on the block. New River Gorge National Park protects and preserves 53 miles of the New River, a waterway that, in its entirety, travels through North Carolina and Virginia before ending in West Virginia. Unlike most North American rivers, New River flows south to north. This park features the longest and deepest river gorge found within the Appalachian Mountains. New River Gorge has both natural and cultural significance, giving visitors a taste of the coal mining life during the eighteenth and nineteenth centuries. New River Gorge Bridge was also the longest steel arch bridge in the world until 2003. Every fall, on the third Saturday in October, festival goers converge to attend Bridge Day, the only day of the year when it is legal to walk on—as well as jump and rappel from—the bridge.

The Bucket List Traveler Tip LOOKING FOR A BASE CAMP FOR YOUR VISIT? STAY IN FAYETTEVILLE. I STAYED AT CANTRELL AND BOOKED MY WHITEWATER RAFTING TRIP WITH THEM. IT WAS A CONVENIENT AND AFFORDABLE OPTION FOR RAFTING AND LODGING, WITH AN ON-SITE RESTAURANT OFFERING FRESH COFFEE EVERY MORNING.

ADVENTURE AWAITS!

DATE(S) VISITED:

TRAVEL COMPANION(S):

WEATHER:

LODGINGS:

NATIONAL PARK PASSPORT STAMP

NATIONAL PARK PASSPORT STAMP

ON THE TRAIL

MY FAVORITE WALKS, HIKES, AND VIEWS

1.   3.

2.   4.

FLORA & FAUNA

THE MOST EXCITING PLANTS AND ANIMALS I SPOTTED ON MY TRIP

1.   3.

2.   4.

TAKE NOTHING BUT MEMORIES

MEMORABLE MOMENTS FROM MY TRIP

PARK RATING ☆ ☆ ☆ ☆ ☆   PLANNING A RETURN TRIP?   YES ☐ NO ☐

NORTH ATLANTIC

It's no secret that what this region lacks in national park count it makes up for in claims to fame. The North Atlantic is home to the first national park to be created east of the Mississippi River, and still the only national park in the Northeast (as of this writing). It is also the only national park created solely from donations of private land to the federal government. The "Crown Jewel of the North Atlantic Coast" protects magnificent coastline unlike any other in the United States and is considered a world-class fall destination when the beautiful forests of maples, aspen, and pines truly come alive. One of the best features of this park is the two-fer: catching the very first sight of sunrise in America from the highest peak along the Maine coast (Cadillac Mountain at 1,530 feet) for half of the year (October to March). Included in this section is the only national park in this region, located in Maine.

Maine

☐ **ACADIA NATIONAL PARK**

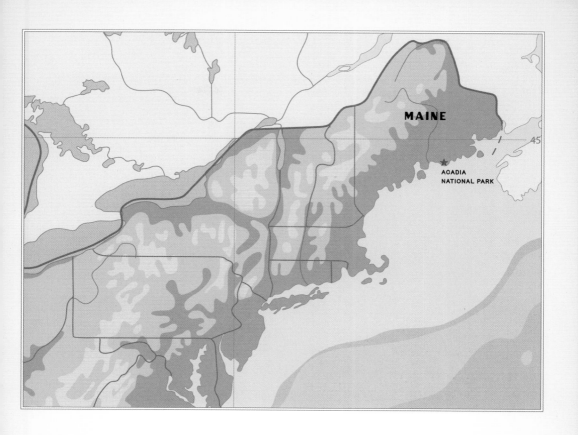

MAINE

45

★
ACADIA
NATIONAL PARK

ACADIA NATIONAL PARK

ESTABLISHED: 1919 (1916) • SIZE: 77 SQUARE MILES • LOCATION: COASTAL MAINE
ANCESTRAL LAND OF THE WABANAKI PEOPLE
FOR MORE INFORMATION: NPS.GOV/ACAD

Craggy coastlines, granite mountains, crashing waves, and jaw-dropping New England fall colors. These are some of the best aspects of Acadia National Park. The park protects natural beauty of the highest rocky headlands along the Atlantic coastline of the United States, an abundance of habitats, and a rich cultural heritage. Though the park may appear small on the map, Acadia encompasses nearly 50,000 acres along Maine's coast. The park was formed thanks to the vision (and donations) of private citizens who anticipated the dangers that overdevelopment would bring to this coastal wonderland. Acadia became the first national park created from private lands gifted to the public through the efforts of conservation-minded citizens. The park consists of three major areas: Mount Desert Island (Bar Harbor and Bass Harbor), Schoodic Peninsula, and Isle au Haut. Many of the park's main attractions are located in Bar Harbor.

The Bucket List Traveler Tip IF YOU'RE LOOKING FOR THAT PERFECT VIEW OF THE ICONIC BAR HARBOR HEAD LIGHTHOUSE, TAKE A BOAT TOUR FOR A GREAT PERSPECTIVE FROM THE WATER. I WENT ON THE NATURE CRUISE WITH BASS HARBOR ISLAND CRUISE AND LEARNED ABOUT MAINE'S FISHING INDUSTRY AS THE CREW HAULED A FEW LOBSTER TRAPS.

ADVENTURE AWAITS!

DATE(S) VISITED:

TRAVEL COMPANION(S):

WEATHER:

LODGINGS:

NATIONAL PARK PASSPORT STAMP

NATIONAL PARK PASSPORT STAMP

ON THE TRAIL

MY FAVORITE WALKS, HIKES, AND VIEWS

1.   3.

2.   4.

FLORA & FAUNA

THE MOST EXCITING PLANTS AND ANIMALS I SPOTTED ON MY TRIP

1.   3.

2.   4.

TAKE NOTHING BUT MEMORIES

MEMORABLE MOMENTS FROM MY TRIP

PARK RATING ☆ ☆ ☆ ☆ ☆   PLANNING A RETURN TRIP?   YES ☐ NO ☐

The Bucket List Traveler Top Ten

Welcome to The Bucket List Traveler's version of the Best of America's Best Idea, based on my personal interests and experiences. This list might be surprising to you, and that is the beauty of the National Parks Bucket List journey—so many parks for us to experience, and so many diverse landscapes for us to enjoy. My list is predominantly influenced by my love of geology, rocks, volcanoes, tropical scenery, and overall colorful views. As you find your parks across the country, I encourage you to jot your Top Ten list on the next page. Friends, family, and even strangers will absolutely ask you what your favorites are and you should be prepared!

1. PETRIFIED FOREST NATIONAL PARK, ARIZONA
2. CAPITOL REEF NATIONAL PARK, UTAH
3. LASSEN VOLCANIC NATIONAL PARK, CALIFORNIA
4. NATIONAL PARK OF AMERICAN SAMOA, AMERICAN SAMOA
5. HAWAI'I VOLCANOES NATIONAL PARK, HAWAI'I
6. HALEAKALĀ NATIONAL PARK, HAWAI'I
7. YELLOWSTONE NATIONAL PARK, IDAHO, MONTANA, AND WYOMING
8. BIG BEND NATIONAL PARK, TEXAS
9. JOSHUA TREE NATIONAL PARK, CALIFORNIA
10. CUYAHOGA VALLEY NATIONAL PARK, OHIO

YOUR TOP TEN

1.

2.

3.

4.

5.

6.

7.

8.

9.

10.

NOTES:

Looking Back

FAVORITE "SMALL PARKS" OF THE 420+ NPS UNITS

FAVORITE BUCKET LIST EXPERIENCES

TOP CAMPGROUNDS OR LODGINGS

FAVORITE ACTIVITIES AT THE PARK

BEST BITES AT THE PARK

WHAT NOT TO DO ON FUTURE PARK VISITS

NEXT STOP: MORE PARKS!

The Bucket List Traveler Top Tips

Kobuk Valley

Kotzebue is a good home base if you're looking to spend more time within this region of Alaska. You can find outfitters that will take you to several other National Park Service sites in the area, like Bering Land Bridge National Preserve, Noatak National Preserve, and Cape Krusenstern National Monument.

Denali

Park buses are a solid option for traveling the park's single road. Tour buses are narrated by onboard naturalists and stop at top sightseeing spots, while transit buses are non-narrated, hop-on, hop-off style, that will take you to the end of the road. Trying to balance the experience and the budget? Pick the transit bus.

Lake Clark

I left Anchorage at 7 a.m. on a commuter plane before hopping on a float plane to Katmai National Park. I returned that afternoon, went to the park's visitor center, and had dinner at the lodge. The next day, I went on a "Fire and Ice" flightseeing tour over Lake Clark. At 5:30 p.m., I boarded the plane back to Anchorage.

Katmai

The best times for bear viewing are July and September, though this is dependent on the temperature of the area. If the river water gets warm sooner than expected, salmon may delay their trip upstream until much later in the summer.

Kenai Fjords

If staying overnight in Seward, catch a cab to your lodging. The next day, hop on the shuttle (Exit Glacier Shuttle or Adventure 60 North) from Seward to visit the Exit Glacier. Go ice climbing with Exit Glacier Guides before you head back to the train depot. No rental car required for this stretch of Alaska!

Wrangell—St. Elias

To avoid renting a car for this trip, take a shuttle to McCarthy. Pick-up location options include Glennallen (Kennicott Shuttle) and Anchorage (Kennicott Wilderness Guides and Copper Spike Transport). If you prefer to drive, GoNorth allows their rental vehicles to be taken beyond paved roads.

Glacier Bay

Only 10 percent of park visitors make it to the land side, but there's plenty to do onshore: the Huna Tribal House, interactive activities with park rangers or tribal members of the Tlingit that make your visit more meaningful, and the beauty of the Forest Trail. Spend a night or two in the Bartlett Cove area.

North Cascades

Mid-July is the best time to hit the trails and take in the alpine view, when snow is off the higher elevation trails. Sahale Arm via Cascade Pass Trail offers an extended high-elevation day hike through subalpine meadows and talus fields to the base of the Sahale Glacier.

Olympic

The park has several trails (Peabody Creek Trail, Madison Falls Trail) and areas (Rialto Beach parking lot to Ellen Creek, beaches between the Hoh and Quinault Reservations near Kalaloch area) where leashed pets are allowed, and its neighbor, Olympic National Forest, generally allows leashed pets on trails.

Mount Rainier

The park is considering a timed-entry system to reduce congestion and impact on popular trails. If you can, visit the park during the weekdays. If the popular spots are crowded, explore White River and check out Reflection Lake and Sunbeam Falls. Carbon River is a great option for its rainforest.

Crater Lake

Visiting in the summer can mean the possibility of forest fires in the area. You can "beat" the smoke haze by going to the lake early in the morning, before the wind picks up, or stay longer at the overlook during the day and wait for the scene to occasionally clear up as the wind blows.

Redwood

Not looking to hike? Drive down Howland Hill Road (10 miles one way). The road is narrow and gets you really close to the trees; you can reach out from your car and touch them. This dirt road, built in 1887, predates the park.

Lassen Volcanic

Take the road less traveled and visit all the different areas on the east side of the park. Butte Lake has a great campground, lake, colorful painted dunes, and cinder cones. Warner Valley is surprisingly tranquil, despite all the bubbling hydrothermal activities. Juniper Lake is peaceful and relatively isolated.

Yosemite

Head to Hetch Hetchy, where two of North America's tallest waterfalls (Tueeulala and Wapama Falls) plummet spectacularly over 1,000-foot granite cliffs. Less than 1 percent of park visitors go to this area, though it's ideal for hiking in spring and fall (summer can be hot due to the trails being exposed to sun).

Kings Canyon

If coming from Sequoia National Park, you may be tempted to skip the world's second-largest tree. Don't! At 268 feet tall and 40 feet in diameter, the General Grant Tree is America's only living monument, a "national shrine" to the men and women of the armed forces who served and gave their lives defending America's freedom.

Sequoia

Want to see the General Sherman Tree without hiking down and back up the steep trail? Visit in winter, when you can park at the smaller parking lot by the roadside, or take the free shuttle in the summer months and exit at this very same stop. The giant is just a short walk away.

Pinnacles

The talus caves are fun to explore when they're not closed for bat colony protection. No advance spelunking experience needed; just bring headlamps or flashlights to help you navigate your way. Check the park website for closure warnings.

Death Valley

When checking weather and temperatures during your park planning session, be sure to enter Furnace Creek as the location instead of Death Valley National Park. The desert floor is usually 10°F to 20°F warmer.

Channel Islands

Get your boat tickets online. If the boat to Anacapa from Ventura Harbor is sold out, check the trip to Anacapa from Oxnard Harbor. The Oxnard boat may not be as big, but it'll still get you to the island and back.

Joshua Tree

To avoid large crowds, take that PTO and visit the park on a Friday. Some of my best times here have been spent on Fridays before the weekend visitors started flocking in. For walk-in campsites, arrive early on Friday morning to find an available spot. Campground check-out time is noon, so hover strategically.

Great Basin

Considering how remote this park is, camping is a solid option for an overnight trip. Arrive early before the weekend to secure a site when going during off-peak season. Wheeler Peak campground is my top choice to help acclimate to the higher elevation before hitting the trails the next day.

Grand Canyon

If visiting in peak season, plan to arrive in the park by Friday or before 9 a.m. on weekends. Stay in the park if you can (there's more availability on Fridays versus the weekend) and wake up early to catch the park shuttle with no crowd.

Petrified Forest

There are several options to join ranger-guided hikes or sign up for classes and trips with the Petrified Forest Field Institute to explore the backcountry. I did a couple of the backcountry trails myself in the winter and practically had the area to myself.

Saguaro

If you plan on hiking, start early. Many of the trails have little to no shade. Short hike? Signal Hill Petroglyph Trail. Cardio hike? Wasson Peak. Long hike? Cactus Forest Trail.

Haleakalā

If you're traveling on a budget, I recommend camping your way through your stay. Besides the campground within park boundaries, a great option is Camp Olowalu by the beach. Hostels like Banana Bungalow are a solid option too.

Hawai'i Volcanoes

If you're here during lava flows, Halema'uma'u crater—with overlooks accessible from the Crater Rim Drive—is where the action is at. Check the park website for eruption information and lava viewing locations. Go early (before sunrise) or really late (after 9 p.m.) for best viewing of the lava lake and its glow.

American Samoa

I recommend hiring a tour guide here to optimize your visit. They can help unlock the complex logistics of traveling to Ta'ū and Ofu Islands while advising you on the best itineraries. The local guide I hired for my trip is no longer in service, but Tour American Samoa comes highly recommended.

Glacier National Park

Wildfires or heavy snow may cause road closures along Going-to-the-Sun Road. I still haven't driven the entirety of that road for these reasons. But don't worry—there's a lot to experience on the east side, beyond stopping at Lake McDonald on the west side for the pretty pebble photo.

Yellowstone

Don't miss these iconic sights: Old Faithful eruption, Grand Prismatic Spring, Grand Canyon of the Yellowstone, and bison in Hayden Valley or Lamar Valley. If you can squeeze in one more stop, make it the travertine terrace at Mammoth Hot Springs. You have a high likelihood of seeing the elk herd.

Grand Teton

Early mornings are ideal to spot bears, moose, coyotes, and other wildlife near Snake River, Mormon Row, and Cascade Canyon. Make the trip affordable by camping and bringing groceries. If tent sites are unavailable, get RV sites and sleep in your vehicle. Camper cabins are solid options when sharing and splitting the cost.

Zion

I hiked Angels Landing and Observation Point in late March without worrying about snow or ice, and I hiked the Narrows (with wet suits looking like Power Rangers) and Watchman Trail (stunning sunset) in late November. You may see snow flurries, making the moment even more magical during your hike (true story).

Bryce Canyon

Hit the red rock jackpot and geek out on this park-hopping excursion: Zion National Park, Cedar Breaks National Monument, Bryce Canyon National Park, Grand Staircase–Escalante National Monument, and squeezing in Pipe Springs National Monument on your way back out for some history and cultural lessons.

Capitol Reef

A trip here is best combined with a visit to Grand Staircase–Escalante. If unable to secure a campsite within the park, the towns of Torrey, Boulder, and Escalante make a perfect base camp to roam between the two parks and beyond (add on Kodachrome Basin State Park and Anasazi State Park Museum).

Canyonlands

If you're not able to secure campsites, Moab makes a great base camp. Hotel prices can be steep during peak season, especially when traveling solo. All the more reason to travel during shoulder season (March, April, September, October)!

Arches

Hop between Arches and Canyonlands to skip the crowd. Enter Arches early in the day to get your hikes in, then exit the park midday when the parking lot starts overflowing. Head to Canyonlands (roughly 30 minutes away) to hike some more before returning to Arches after 4 p.m., when you won't need the timed-entry ticket.

Mesa Verde

Ongoing closures on trails and dwellings are to be expected. Park staff always put safety first, so please manage your expectations when visiting. Purchase tour tickets prior to visiting and check the park's website for updated conditions. Tickets are available at Recreation.gov up to two weeks ahead of tour date.

Black Canyon

Painted Wall, the tallest cliff in Colorado, is 2,250 feet tall from river to rim. While the Painted Wall View Overlook is as close as you'd get when staying on the rim, the Cedar Point Nature Trail takes you to a picture-perfect view of the Painted Wall in its entirety, rim to river.

Rocky Mountain

Moraine Park just after sunrise offers your best chance to spot bugling elk. From May to August, you can view bighorn sheep at Sheep Lakes and catch a glimpse of the elusive moose population along the Colorado River in Kawuneeche Valley. Remember to leave wildlife wild and view them from a safe distance.

Great Sand Dunes

Although not quite within the park boundaries, Zapata Falls is too close to not chase the waterfalls. The falls are rather unique, tucked back in a short rock tunnel where water funnels 30 feet down from the creek high above. Best views are under the shower of the falls.

Theodore Roosevelt

If you're like me, struggling to balance conservation while embracing #LandBack, consider acknowledging that our parks are indeed dynamic. A fuller representation of human history—and for this park, of Roosevelt and his views of Indigenous peoples as barriers to conservation—would paint a more complete picture. Keep an open mind and keep relearning.

Wind Cave

For the rebels out there, rejoice! Wind Cave is an open-hike park, meaning visitors are welcome to hike off designated trails aboveground (which is very uncommon at national parks). Pack plenty of water and a map, and be aware of your surroundings and wildlife.

Badlands

The park often gets the reputation of an "interstate park," where you exit off I-90 and drive through the park, snap some photos, use the bathroom, then leave without much trip planning or having some dirt (or some days, mud) on your shoes. Don't let this be you.

Hot Springs

Experience what each historic bathhouse has to offer. Buckstaff and Quapaw operate as bathhouses. Hale is a luxury hotel. Superior is a modern-day brewery, the only kind to utilize thermal spring water to make their beer. Ozark houses the Hot Springs National Park Cultural Center. Lamar is used as the park's resources management office and store.

Carlsbad

If the thought of descending into the cavern via the "natural entrance" is daunting, you can take the elevator inside the visitor center to travel 754 feet down, arriving by the Underground Lunchroom before you start your cave exploration at the Big Room.

White Sands

This park sits on one of the largest military bases in the United States, the White Sands Missile Range. This means sometimes the park is closed due to missile tests. Be sure to check the park's website before heading out.

Big Bend

A hybrid of inside and outside park accommodation is a good compromise. I camped at Stillwell Store and RV Park, 8 miles away from the Persimmon Gap Visitor Center, and spent my first few days on the desert floor. When I was able to secure a campsite at Chisos Basin Campground, I spent the rest of my trip there.

Guadalupe Mountains

If you're into peak bagging, there are seven more of Texas's highest peaks located inside the park: Bush Mountain (8,631 feet), Shumard Peak (8,615 feet), Bartlett Peak (8,508 feet), Hunter Peak (8,368 feet), Mount Pratt (8,342 feet), El Capitan (8,085 feet), and Lost Peak (7,818 feet). Join the Great 8 Peak Challenge and bag them all!

Indiana Dunes

I've visited Indiana Dunes on Memorial Day and Labor Day. Unless you're planning to take a swim in the lake, I highly recommend visiting in late springtime (May was perfect) for cooler weather and blooming wildflowers. The park was surprisingly not that crowded during both holiday visits.

Isle Royale

Don't miss Grand Portage National Monument. This small park is located 2 miles from Hat Point Ferry Terminal where you board *Sea Hunter III* to Isle Royale. Here, you can learn about the partnership between the Grand Portage Anishinaabe tribe and the North West Company during the North American fur trade.

Voyageurs

Fan of Smokey Bear? His giant statue stands 26 feet tall at Smokey Bear Park in International Falls, Minnesota. The cartoon character was invented during World War II to protect the nation's lumber resources from careless campfires, and is now managed by the US Forest Service.

Cuyahoga Valley

The Conservancy for Cuyahoga Valley National Park has a program called "Sponsor an Acre" and I think it's the most brilliant way to fundraise money while making it meaningful to donors. You can sponsor an acre in your favorite spot or gift a sponsored acre to a loved one (100 percent tax deductible).

Biscayne

Don't confuse Biscayne National Park with the state park in Key Biscayne (Bill Baggs Cape Florida State Park). The parks are 46 miles away from each other. The state park (affectionately referred to as Key Biscayne) is located on the northern end of Biscayne Bay, home to Cape Florida Lighthouse.

Dry Tortugas

If I could redo my first trip here, I'd either spend the night before in Key West or fork over the funds to take the seaplane. The night before the trip, I stayed in Fort Lauderdale, necessitating a super early wake-up time. No amount of coffee was enough, and I arrived almost on time.

Everglades

Look for flamingos at the Flamingo area by Flamingo Beach or by Snake Bight area in Florida Bay. The best time of year to see these beautiful birds is in the spring, late March to early May, as they prefer the more favorable weather. To see creatures with more bite, take the Shark Valley Tram Tour for a relaxing visit and safely navigate around the gators.

Mammoth Cave

The park sits on the far eastern side of the Central Time Zone (GMT-5). If you're coming from the north side or the Eastern Time Zone, it can be quite confusing. Be aware of your time zones as you cross them so you don't miss your cave tour.

Great Smoky Mountains

Though technically not within park boundaries, Mingo Falls in the Qualla Boundary just outside the park is not to be missed. It's a short hike with some staircases, but the view is absolutely worth heavy breathing for. At 120 feet tall, this waterfall is one of the tallest and most spectacular in the southern Appalachians.

Congaree

Though the park has suspended their Wilderness Canoe Tours as of this writing, there are local outfitters that operate tours and/or rent equipment. I booked a guided canoe trip (you can book kayak too) with Palmetto Outdoor. Highly recommend!

Virgin Islands

Deciding the adventure level you want at this park will help determine your trip logistics (camping, hotel, Airbnb, rental car or taxi, etc.). I did a tour with Virgin Islands Ecotours, where I hiked from the visitor center to Honeymoon Bay for a guided kayak and snorkel trip.

Shenandoah

The two northern park entrances are almost always busy with long lines. Plan to use the two southern entrances (Swift Run and Rockfish) for shorter wait times.

New River Gorge

The best spots for sunrise are at Long Point Trail and Grandview Main Overlook. For sunset, the New River Gorge Bridge Overlook by Canyon Rim Visitor Center, Endless Wall Trail, and Sandstone Falls Overlook are all solid choices.

Acadia

In search of fall color and feeling adventurous? Hike up the Beehive Trail (less strenuous than the Precipice Trail) and enjoy the magnificent views from up top. Pack some snacks and stay as long as you like to enjoy the views.

Resources

Websites

Parks' Campground and Lodging Information: www.thebucketlisttraveler.com

National Park System (420+ Units/Parks List): www.nps.gov/aboutus/national-park-system.htm

Find a Park: www.nps.gov/findapark/advanced-search.htm

Find a National Park Service Map: www.nps.gov/planyourvisit/maps.htm

Plan Like a Park Ranger: www.nps.gov/aboutus/news/plan-like-a-park-ranger.htm

Park Reservation and Timed-Entry Systems: www.npca.org/reports/know-before-you-go

Annual Events at the Parks: www.nps.gov/subjects/npscelebrates/annual-events.htm

Recreate Responsibly: www.nps.gov/planyourvisit/recreate-responsibly.htm

Kids in the Parks: www.nps.gov/kids/index.htm

Become a Junior Ranger: www.nps.gov/kids/become-a-junior-ranger.htm

Find Your "Virtual" Park: www.nps.gov/subjects/npscelebrates/find-your-virtual-park.htm

My Park Story Podcast Series: www.nps.gov/subjects/npscelebrates/your-park-story.htm

Discover the History of the NPS: www.nps.gov/history/index.htm

Telling All Americans' Stories: Publications on Diverse and Inclusive History:
www.nps.gov/articles/publications-diverse.htm

National Park Foundation Blog: www.nationalparks.org/stories

Explore America's National Parks: www.nationalparks.org/explore/parks

National Park Geek Instagram for Photos and Park Inspiration:
www.instagram.com/nationalparkgeek

Watch *The National Parks*, a film by Ken Burns: www.pbs.org/kenburns/the-national-parks/

Books

Your Guide to the National Parks by Michael Joseph Oswald
The Dayhiker's Guide to the National Parks by Michael Joseph Oswald
National Park Maps Atlas by Michael Joseph Oswald
Moon USA National Parks by Becky Lomax

National Park Service Social Media

Facebook: Receive updates, news releases, photos, videos, events, and live streams from parks and NPS programs. Share your park photos, videos, and experiences with them and the rest of the national park loving online community. www.facebook.com/nationalparkservice

Instagram: Get your daily inspiration of photos, videos, and live stories from parks around the country. www.instagram.com/nationalparkservice/

X (Twitter): Receive park updates, news releases, photos, and videos from @NatlParkService. www.twitter.com/natlparkservice

Flickr: Discover high quality, full-resolution public domain images. www.flickr.com/photos/nationalparkservice

LinkedIn: Learn about internships, careers, and working with the National Park Service. www.linkedin.com/company/national-park-service/

YouTube: Explore videos about wildlife, history, events, trip planning, and more. www.youtube.com/nationalparkservice

ACKNOWLEDGMENTS

• • •

Writing a book on national parks was a "someday" bucket list item of mine, so to actually publish one this year is a major bucket list item checked. So much gratitude goes to my team at Quarto (Rage, Nicole, Katie, Lori, and Steve) for the opportunity to author this book and the trust, care, and patience you have shown me as I go through this book-writing and publishing process for the very first time.

Although my National Parks Bucket List journey started with me as a solo traveler, my kind, thoughtful, and supportive husband, Karey, has been with me every step of the way during this book-writing process. Thank you, love, for the daily coffee runs when I was deep in the trenches typing away through many late nights for this journal to come to fruition, and for reaffirming my vision and aptitude.

To the National Park Geek family and The Bucket List Traveler community, many thanks for the inspiration and continued friendship through the years, for the trips, chats, stories shared, photos exchanged, and memories made. Thank you for being a part of my core memories and realizing my American dream. To my dear friend Kelsi, I'm so grateful for you. Thank you for being a part of my support system from day one of this book project.

And to you, reading this book and journaling your way through America's Best Idea, I appreciate you dearly. I hope our paths cross someday on the trails or at the visitor center.

Happy Trails,
Linda Mohammad
@thebucketlisttraveler

ABOUT THE AUTHOR

· · ·

Linda Mohammad is a national park lover and self-proclaimed weekend warrior. Originally born and raised in Malaysia, she migrated to the United States in pursuit of her engineering degrees at Colorado School of Mines. Her passion for traveling stemmed from the good old college days when she'd have to vacate her dorm room during school breaks. The love for national parks later sparked when she first attended geology field trips as part of her graduate school syllabus. Fast-forward to today, Linda is an engineer working in the energy industry and California is her home base. She serves as a volunteer in park (VIP) for the National Park Service and is an executive board member for the Channel Islands Park Foundation, a philanthropic group for California's Channel Islands National Park. She is known as The Bucket List Traveler who journals her way through the parks, and documenting her visits, hiking, trip planning, storytelling, and list-making are her forte. On the weekends, she can be found exploring some of our many national parks across the country. To date, she has checked off all 63 big national parks in the United States and more than half of the 420+ national park units managed by the National Park Service. Follow along on her adventures at www.thebucketlisttraveler.com.

First published in 2024 by Epic Ink, an imprint of The Quarto Group,
142 West 36th Street, 4th Floor, New York, NY 10018, USA
T (212) 779-4972 www.Quarto.com

Epic Ink titles are also available at discount for retail, wholesale,
promotional, and bulk purchase. For details, contact the Special Sales
Manager by email at specialsales@quarto.com or by mail at The Quarto
Group, Attn: Special Sales Manager, 100 Cummings Center Suite 265D,
Beverly, MA 01915 USA.

10 9 8 7 6 5 4 3 2 1

ISBN: 978-0-76038-681-1

Group Publisher: Rage Kindelsperger
Editorial Director: Lori Burke
Creative Director: Laura Drew
Managing Editor: Cara Donaldson
Editor: Katie McGuire
Cover Design: Beth Middleworth
Interior Design: Beth Middleworth/Rebecca Pagel
Ilustrations: Aloysius Patrimonio/Shutterstock

Printed in China

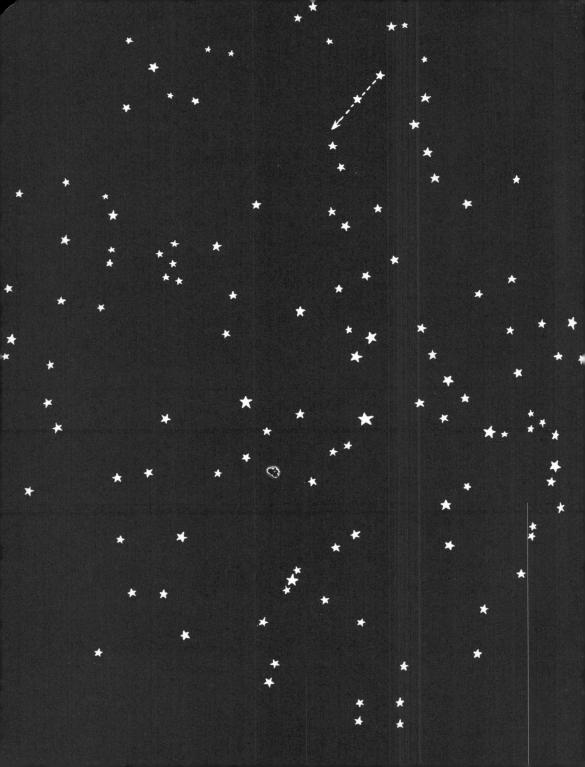